TOUCHED BY A HERO

*A 9/11 Widow's Journal
of Love & Legacy*

The statue of Rick Rescorla, created by sculptor Edward Hlavka, was unveiled in 2006 at Fort Benning, Georgia.

TOUCHED BY A HERO

A 9/11 Widow's Journal of Love & Legacy

By Susan Rescorla

With David Sandler

Foreword By William J. Bennett
Former United States Secretary of Education

Published By:
The Richard C. Rescorla Memorial

ISBN-13: 978-1461098546

Library of Congress Control Number: 2011910721

Published By:
The Richard C. Rescorla Memorial

Books available at:
www.amazon.com
www.createspace.com
www.rickrescorla.com

PRINTED IN THE UNITED STATES OF AMERICA BY CREATESPACE

To my Rick
and
all the 9/11 Heroes

Contents

Foreword

In an age when heroes come and go too quickly, it is important we remember them, learn from them, teach about them, and make them more permanent. Rick Rescorla is such a hero.

Born in England, he fought for and saved Americans. From Vietnam to 9/11, Rick Rescorla joined the league of American immigrants who helped teach us what it should mean to be an American — and what an American hero is. Today, there is a statue of Rick at Fort Benning, one of his favorite places. But there should be a statue of him in New York, too. It was there, as a civilian, as Morgan Stanley's Second Vice President for Corporate Security at the World Trade Center, that he spent his last years, and was spent in his final year. He knew, better than most, the target the World Trade Center could be for terrorists, and he drove his colleagues nuts practicing evacuation strategies for years before 9/11. But most of them are alive today because of those efforts. When that dreadful day did come, he died while helping others escape. His last recorded words were, "As soon as I make sure everyone else gets out."

He said those words in response to Morgan Stanley regional manager John Olson, who was yelling at him: "Rick, you've got to get out, too!"

When I discussed his life on my radio show, I had callers from across the country who knew him personally, and a few whom he mentored — they remembered him telling them and counseling them to straighten out their lives which they had been neglecting through substance abuse and sloth. He saved those lives, too, and his former mentees know it. There are Americans alive today because this American by choice dedicated his life to them. While we venerate too many not deserving the title "hero" today, we neglect the real ones, the ones we can learn from. The ones we should emulate. The ones we should hold up. Rick Rescorla is such a hero.

William J. Bennett
Former United States Secretary of Education

TOUCHED BY A HERO

*A 9/11 Widow's Journal
of Love & Legacy*

Awakening to Healing

"There are many words to describe that terrible day. Among them, is the single word COURAGE. On a day when courage was the absolute rule, the courage of a few, would be the dominant feature. Colonel Rick Rescorla was one of them. It has been my honor to help honor his memory. He was the greatest man, I never knew."

U.S. Air Force Master Sgt. Mike "Bearman" Angelastro (Ret.)

*R*oar! The sound of over 100 people revving their motorcycle engines is ear shattering, scary and exhilarating. I am sitting on Mike "Bearman" Angelastro's Harley-Davidson, holding onto him tightly. This is definitely not my usual scene, although I have been a passenger on a motorcycle twice before and recall loving the ride both times. This ride is about to begin on a rainy, foggy, early

Saturday morning, September 12, 2009, and my adrenaline is soaring.

More than 100 men (and several women) are gathered for a 1,000-mile journey from Floyd Bennett Field in Brooklyn, New York, to Fort Benning, Georgia. We are transporting a two-ton, 12-foot long steel beam, recovered from the World Trade Center that was demolished by terrorists on September 11, 2001.

Mike is the Lead Run Coordinator for the Iron and Steel Blue Team, part of the "Iron and Steel — NYC to Fort Benning Run," organized by the FDNY Fire Family Transport Foundation. I will be riding with Mike and retired firefighter Rich Snyder during the run.

The I-Beam lies on a flatbed truck driven by retired New York Fire Department Lieutenant Pat "Paddy" Concannon, who is the Foundation's president and founding member, and retired firefighter Danny Prince. Another flatbed transports a fire engine called "Fire Engine #343," representing the 343 firefighters murdered that day, driven by Foundation member and former U.S. Marine Mike Stallone.

A filmmaker, photographer, and founder of Sundland Productions, Barbara Lang-Auffret, daughter of a retired New York Police detective, and niece of a retired FDNY firefighter, is also on this ride. Barbara had traveled to several states to film memorials erected to honor 9/11 victims. As Barbara put it:

> All the bits and pieces I had locked inside were like a grand puzzle with pieces scattered about until I contacted Mike Angelastro, the Ride Coordinator for the Iron & Steel. I knew the group was planning to bring steel from the towers to their brothers at the Shanksville Volunteer Fire Company, the first responders when Flight 93 crashed in a field after

passengers tried to overtake the terrorists. I suggested he think about bringing the next piece of steel to Fort Benning to honor Rick Rescorla, who saved so many on 9/11, and gave his life so that others may live. Certainly, everyone had heard of the bravery, heroism and love that Rick Rescorla demonstrated for others on 9/11, in his quest as a military man to leave no man behind.

One day I received a call from Mike letting me know his group planned to bring the steel beam to Fort Benning. As we talked, I realized that this was something I deeply wanted to be involved with. Although I would never have imagined participating in a 1,000-mile motorcycle trip to anywhere, I found myself telling Mike I wanted to be involved, attend meetings and ride down with them. Our conversation, nearly eight years after 9/11, began the healing that helped me to expand my capacity to feel the loss not only of my dear husband, but also for the many others murdered that day — and reawaken to my life.

I had been unable to focus on much more than my grief over the loss of Rick all these years, but taking part in this ride proved to be a turning point. At my first meeting, I established a closeness with the group immediately. I realized that patriotism was alive and well in the hearts of these firefighters, military veterans, police officers and others coming together for this wonderful tribute. Bringing the steel beam to Fort Benning was not only a tribute to the 9/11 victims, but also an honor to those fighting, and sadly, still dying for our country.

I spoke about how much bringing the steel beam down to Fort Benning meant to me, that I believed the souls of all the 9/11 victims were contained on the piece of steel.

"The ride to Fort Benning is a sacred act," I said.

The steel beam was to be added to a 9/11 tribute display at Fort Benning, near a statue of my husband, Retired Army Colonel Cyril Richard Rescorla, who was murdered in the 9/11 attacks. Rick graduated from Fort Benning Officer Candidate School, and in April 2001, inducted into its OCS Hall of Fame. The remarkable bronze statue of Rick was unveiled during a beautiful ceremony in 2006, to honor his heroism in both 9/11 and Vietnam.

I recently learned that shortly after talking with Mike that first time, he told Iron and Steel Team Director Greg "Spock" Alspach that I wanted to be part of the ride, and Spock said, "Susan Rescorla, as in Rick Rescorla's widow?"

"Yes, she's coming with us on the run," Mike replied.

"Practical question," said Spock. "Does she ride?"

"I don't think so bro'," Mike said. "But I don't think that's going to stop her."

Mike was right, and it did not take Spock long to understand my determination. As Spock recently noted:

> Despite what had to be, at least at moments, a painful emotional subject matter, Susan jumped right in with both feet. The Iron and Steel riders attract attention like rock stars on the road, but we're traveling on motorcycles. It was a joy to have Susan with us. She was the Energizer Bunny of the Iron and Steel Run. Though I never knew Rick in life, getting to know Susan and other family members and friends, I can feel Susan's sadness and understand her reasons for keeping up the good fight. I have always been a sucker for a triumph

from tragedy story. Susan Rescorla is a National Treasure. My hat is off to you.

I remember having mixed emotions while packing the night before in my Mendham, New Jersey home. I tried to imagine what Rick would think about what I was doing. A war hero, awarded a Silver Star, Bronze Star, Purple Heart, and Vietnamese Cross of Gallantry, Rick always rejected the hero label.

"The real heroes are dead," he said.

In fact, Rick refused to let me display his military medals, awards and certificates in our home. But now, eight years after the horrific event that forever changed my life, my mind was clearing. With the tremendous support of so many others, I had been doing all I could since 9/11 to keep his legacy of courage, honor and love alive. Participating in this ride, bringing the steel beam to the place of honor it deserved, allowed me to transcend my personal loss, and provide some degree of closure.

A coordinator of the event had forewarned participants that the ride from Brooklyn, through New Jersey, Pennsylvania, Maryland, West Virginia, North Carolina, South Carolina and Georgia, would be challenging. Summed up in the organizer's "participate but be prepared" message, we were told that September was peak hurricane season, and even without storms or weather fronts, afternoon "pop up" showers, created by the heat of the day, were not uncommon. We were leaving New York, where temperatures were in the lows 40s, but our route would lead us to weather with temperatures over 100 degrees. We were advised to bring sun block, wear light colored, cotton, long-sleeved shirts, drink plenty of water, and keep our caffeine and alcohol intake to a minimum to avoid dehydration. Rick would have called it a simple case of following the Eight P's, drilled into his psyche during his military years —"Proper prior planning and preparation prevents piss-poor performance."

We left Floyd Bennett Field in a deafening roar of engines and approached the Verrazano-Narrows Bridge, which I did not realize had been closed to traffic for our convoy. I looked off into the Hudson and noticed a fireboat shooting its water guns high into the air in honor of our mission as we passed by.

At this early stage of the ride, the fog was low and eerie. The weather reminded me of my first trip to Ground Zero with my daughter Aly, about three weeks after 9/11. I was still in such shock, I couldn't remember much. I do recall a hint of white smoke remained where the Twin Towers once stood. Bits of paper were still floating in the wind. I could not view this as the place where Rick died. Ground Zero was the place where my husband was murdered. Now he was gone, flying with the eagles that he so admired.

Rick was murdered at a time when life held so much promise for both of us. In fact we celebrated our closeness by renewing our vows within a year in Rick's birthplace of Cornwall, England.

Renewal of Vows

We, Richard Rescorla and Susan Rescorla, husband and wife, lovers and companions, travelers from across the sea, have been blown by a sacred wind to this old Norman church. Standing in this holy garden, we affirm our wedding vows in the presence of our Celtic ancestors who sleep in peace in the graveyard on the sand dunes nearby.

We perform this ceremony with all humility, knowing that we do not stand an inch higher than the lowliest of God's creatures. As we confirm our love for each other, we also unite two divine rivers of thought: the faith in a great creator is bonded to the belief in the eternal harmony of the spheres.

May our love be renewed each day, shining as bright as the beautiful stained glass windows of this church. At this moment we feel the wonder of nature, a sense of unity with the earth, the sky, the sea, the lichen-covered rocks. Songbirds sit on the branches above us. We hear the music of a robin calling for her mate.

The blossoming Hawthorne tree nearby reminds us of the natural and orderly course of time. We are aware that our time on earth is brief: the footprints that we make in this sandy soil will one day be washed away by an eternal tide. Our souls will then go forth, arm in arm, on an everlasting journey.

As the mist rises above the river we hold hands and count our blessings. We ask the pink and white wildflowers that surround us, and every leaf of grass, to witness our vows and celebrate our happiness.

We give ourselves to each other for all eternity, for better or worse, in sickness or in health, and in this instance seek the blessing of a merciful God.

St. Unys Church
Lelant, Kernow
May 2000

Rick had been contemplating retirement. He was continually searching for and beginning to find peace in a life that had been so close to the brutality of war in Vietnam, in addition to a lifetime of security work, including: an intelligence unit in Cyprus during the Cypriot insurgency; a paramilitary police inspector of the Northern Rhodesia Police (now called the Zambia Police Service); one of Scotland Yard's "Flying Squad" of detectives as a member of London's Metropolitan Police; work with Continental Illinois National Bank and Trust Company in Chicago, and his last 14 years as Morgan Stanley's Second Vice President for Corporate Security. He said he was feeling centered and good about life. About four years before his murder, he was diagnosed with prostate cancer, and it had spread into his bones. At the time his doctors gave him six months to live, but through a combination of standard treatments and a holistic approach, including herbal medicine, the cancer was in remission. In fact, he recently learned from his doctor that his latest PSA Test had come back at zero, and amazingly, cancer could longer be detected in his bone marrow.

"I know I'm going to live past 70, and I'm going to kick this cancer," he told me.

It was difficult to hold back my tears as we rode. I was so proud to be a part of this ride. The roar of the motorcycles was loud, still somewhat unnerving, at least to me, but thrilling. I continued holding on, probably too tight to Mike. I noticed that at nearly every overpass, groups of people surrounded by fire engines and cars were waving American flags and saluting, cheering us on.

My husband's death had turned my life upside down, and not only for the obvious reasons. The role Rick played on 9/11 for Morgan Stanley in getting all but 13 of the firm's nearly 2,700 employees out of the South Tower alive received worldwide attention. Morgan Stanley was the World Trade Center's largest tenant, occupying 21 floors between the 43rd and 74th floors of the South Tower. Looking out from his office on the 44th floor, Rick saw the fires raging in the North Tower after it was hit by hijacked American Airlines Flight 11. He also heard the announcements over the intercom from The Port Authority, owners of the World Trade Center, reassuring South Tower employees of their safety and advising them to remain in their offices and cubicles.

Rick thought otherwise. With bullhorn in hand, Rick reportedly moved between floors, ordering people to leave the building immediately, just as they had practiced for several years during the evacuation drills he had insisted on over the years. When the second plane, United Airlines Flight 175, crashed into the South Tower between floors 77 and 85, Morgan Stanley employees maintained their brisk, but steady pace, pairing up as trained, and safely walking down the 44-inch wide staircase. Rick helped employees remain as calm as possible by singing military songs through his bullhorn to accompany their descent. He reportedly urged people on, declaring: "Today is a day to be proud to be an American, tomorrow the world will be looking at you."

When all his people were safely evacuated, Rick, Morgan Stanley Deputy Wesley Mercer, security guards Godwin Forde and Jorge Velasquez went back up the stairs to see who else needed help. Moments later, the South Tower collapsed, Rick, and his three men were presumably crushed to death.

Most Morgan Stanley employees credit Rick's insistence to train them in evacuation procedures as the reason for their safe escape. From Rick's perspective, I think he would say he was just doing his job. Shortly after being hired by the firm in 1987, he warned his employer that the World

Trade Center's underground truck entrance was a "soft target" and vulnerable to attack. After the 1993 detonation of a truck bomb in the garage, he told his close friend Dan Hill, who had done security consulting for him, "damn it, they didn't listen to me."

Rick clearly understood that a new form of terrorism had begun, and urged Morgan Stanley to move to another location. With help from Dan and his other closest friend, Fred McBee, "Team Rescorla," as they called themselves, outlined potential future terrorist attacks, including detailed computer flight simulations of planes flying into the Twin Towers. Team Rescorla was already referring to the World Trade Center as "Ground Zero." Rick turned in a report warning officials that the next strike would be by air. Despite Rick's urging of the Port Authority to do more to protect the World Trade Center from attack, his warnings were for the most part dismissed.

So Rick did what he could do, and managed to convince Morgan Stanley to allow him to design and implement mandatory, surprise evacuation training drills. He had generators and stair lighting installed in case of power failure, assigned "fire warden" responsibilities to some people, and insisted that everyone, even top Morgan Stanley executives, take part in the drills, whether or not they were in the midst of a multimillion-dollar transaction. Despite some skepticism regarding the need for evacuation drills, which took place every few months, people complied, and as a result, safely exited the South Tower in a relatively orderly manner. In January 2011, I received an email from a Morgan Stanley employee expressing his gratitude to Rick.

My name is Josh Mattox — I am a Morgan Stanley employee. I was a survivor of 9/11. I was on the 61st floor. At the time

I was 21 years old and just out of college — my whole life ahead of me! Thanks to your husband that life is going forward. I have the opportunity to get married, have children and watch my parents age — for all these things I am VERY thankful. I have thanked your husband many times in my prayers for the opportunities he gave me. Without his courage and wisdom I have no doubt I would have died that day.

The emergence of details about his foresight and role on 9/11 raised public awareness of Rick. In addition to newspaper and magazine stories, Simon & Schuster published *Heart of a Soldier, A Story of Love, Heroism, and September 11th*, written by Pulitzer Prize winning author James B. Stewart. A video entitled *The Voice of the Prophet* consisting solely of Rick describing his terrorist concerns from his Morgan Stanley office, was premiered at the Sundance Film Festival, and shown at the Toronto, and Human Rights Watch Film Festivals. A History Channel documentary, *The Man Who Predicted 9/11*, featuring Rick as "one of the unsung heroes of 9/11," was broadcast on September 11, 2005, and continues to run periodically, particularly on the anniversary of 9/11.

Most recently, the San Francisco Opera premiered a new work by composer Christopher Theofanidis and librettist Donna DiNovelli at the War Memorial Opera House on September 10, 2011, the eve of the 10th anniversary of 9/11, based on *Heart of a Soldier*. The opera, directed by Francesca Zambello and conducted by Patrick Summers, starred baritone Thomas Hampson singing the role of Rick, the soprano Melody Moore singing my role, and the part of Dan Hill sung by tenor William Burden.

Rick's heroism was no surprise to those who knew him best,

particularly the men who fought with him in Vietnam. Although he left the Army in July 1966 with serious doubts about U.S. objectives there, Rick's leadership and courage in Vietnam was legendary and his men called him "Hard Core." A Second Lieutenant, Rick was in the 1st Platoon, Bravo Company, 2nd Battalion, 7th Cavalry, and played a pivotal role in the army's first major engagement in Vietnam, the Battle of Ia Drang Valley, on November 14, 1965. His battalion's experience was chronicled in the book *We Were Soldiers Once . . . and Young*, written by Lieutenant General Hal Moore (Ret.), and reporter Joseph L. Galloway, who were both there. A gripping photo of Rick with his rifle raised, slightly crouched, ready to spring to action was captured by photojournalist Peter Arnett and used for the book's cover.

When Rick was murdered, I was unexpectedly swept into a public role that took me by surprise. The day after 9/11, I was bombarded by the media, and over the years have been interviewed by dozens of reporters, made several radio and television appearances, including *Dateline NBC*, with co-host Jane Pauley, been interviewed in my home by correspondents from Japan, Hungary, Italy and Great Britain, and asked to speak to small and large groups on many occasions. To meet these requests, I had little choice but to bury my grief to whatever extent possible in order to function.

The "Iron and Steel — NYC to Fort Benning Run," was the catalyst to help me feel the grief others were also experiencing, and to deepen my appreciation and awareness of the remarkable impact Rick has had on so many. September 11th may have been the last chapter of Rick's heroic life, but this 1,000-mile journey helped transform me from someone traumatized by the loss of my husband, to someone ready to resume my life and honor Rick's legacy of courage.

On the first night of the ride, we stayed in Martinsburg, West Virginia. Paddy had identified a nearby military airbase that would secure the steel beam overnight. An American flag was draped over the steel and a light mounted to shine down on it until the next morning, when a few people gathered while an officer from the base solemnly folded the flag and gave it to Paddy. When I learned from Paddy of how the steel beam had been secured, I felt chills, spiritual chills. The steel was being treated with the respect and dignity one would observe towards a dead person.

As the ride progressed over the next few days, with stops at fire stations, a Harley-Davidson dealership, rest stops and hotels, I recognized a look of awe from many when they saw the steel beam. Some were moved to tears, and people were genuinely pleased when we encouraged them to write a few words on the beam, or place their hands on the piece of steel. Heading into Georgia, heavy rain poured down. Many riders told me later that if we had not been in a cavalcade, they would have pulled over and waited until the rain lightened up. Yet, despite the conditions, we could not stop. I think Paddy Concannon summed up our feelings when he told a reporter, "By the time we hit Georgia, we had 20 state police in front, we had squad cars on either side, we had people on overpasses, we had American flags off pick-up trucks. It was the most patriotic, inspirational thing that I think I've ever experienced."

There was a place for us to stop shortly after we entered Georgia to eat and relax. The rain was still pouring down. My dear friend, Nick Snider, welcomed us and to my surprise had erected a booth to honor Rick. Nick was an Officer Candidate School graduate himself, and founder of the National Museum of Patriotism in Atlanta. Many people on the ride were unfamiliar with Rick's heroism before 9/11. The booth

13

Nick set up included pictures of Rick, military memorabilia, and written information about his valor under fire.

The unveiling of the steel beam ceremony was beautiful, and Rick's children, Kim and Trevor, flew down to attend. The firefighters and military personnel were dressed in formal attire. The Fannin County Middle School choir sang. Fort Benning Commanding General, Major General Michael Ferriter, compared the steel beam to our soldiers, and said it was only appropriate that it be located at Fort Benning near the statue of Rick, to inspire future generations of soldiers.

"Good leaders inspire others to follow, but great leaders inspire others to lead, and Rick Rescorla was an example of a great leader," said General Ferriter.

Kim, Trevor, Paddy and I were asked to come forward to unveil the steel beam. That was a very emotional moment for all of us. Then we all shared a meal and it was a quick goodbye, as everyone was quite exhausted by this point. While not wanting the experience to end, I could feel the healing taking place inside of me in the community of others.

Soon after my return home, I wrote in my journal:

It is the beginning of Fall and for some reason, I am more aware of the change this year. The change in me. I feel like I am wearing a cloak to keep me warm, it is made from a mantle of leaves that are gold and purple, red and green and yellow. As I step out into my imaginary world, I shall try to keep on my path. Now and again and again, reaching for an adventure of my own, and then coming back again, on the path, reaching for more.

The effects of the trauma of 9/11, the media attention, speeches, and travel, while certainly not gone, was continuing to diminish. Thinking back to Rick, the man I knew was a fun loving, fiercely intelligent person. He had done so much during his life, earning bachelor and master degrees at the University of Oklahoma, obtaining his law degree from the Oklahoma City University School of Law, in addition to his military and security work. He was a voracious reader, devouring everything from classic literature and historical nonfiction, to tales of the Wild West. He could speak several languages. Rick was writing a script with the writer Jim Morris, who he had met at the University of Oklahoma, about World War II legend Audie Murphy, that he hoped to have produced. Rick was also writing his autobiography. He was at a good point in life, where he was sorting out his place in the world.

We met during a chance encounter. I was walking my dear dog Buddy, when out of nowhere this large man, barefoot no less, ran by.

"What are you doing jogging in your bare feet?" I instinctively called out. Slowing down a bit, he said he needed to get the feel of what it was like to run without shoes to help him be more informed for a play he was writing set in Africa.

I was a woman in her 50s at the time, with three grown daughters and two failed marriages. He was a man, also in his 50s, with two grown children, and divorced after a 22-year marriage. If such a thing exists as love at first sight, our chance meeting that day evolved into a whirlwind romance, culminating in an intimate marriage ceremony on February 20, 1999, at Castillo de San Marcos in St. Augustine, Florida. The location was where his close friend Dan Hill and wife Pat lived, and it reminded Rick of his seaside childhood home in Hayle, England. My life felt whole again. Marrying Rick Rescorla was the best thing that ever happened to me. A question I asked my mother after my second divorce — did she think anyone would ever love me again — had been answered.

We were only together for three years, yet we were inseparable. We just had fun, and knew we had finally met our soulmate. He told me how he would notice the tight lips and stressed look on so many people's faces walking off the train following the commute from Manhattan to Morristown at the end of the day. Yet "I still felt good," he said. In that regard, I think I helped him a lot. When I asked him what do you love most about me, he said it was my spirit because I could lift him up in a minute.

Our lives were filled with spontaneous trips to art galleries, antique shops, parks, historic sites, and sometimes — just long rides along the Delaware Water Gap, which cuts through a large ridge of the Appalachian Mountains on the New Jersey and Pennsylvania border. We took yoga and ballroom dancing classes together. We loved to travel, with trips to upstate New York, Cape Cod, a magical week in Sante Fe, New Mexico, and two visits to Cornwall, the first for our honeymoon, the second to renew our vows. Rick was reading about Zen Buddhism, teaching me about the value of meditation, and felt optimistic about his health. I knew from the moment I met him that he was the most fabulous man in the whole world and I was so lucky to have him in my life.

Then, on September 11, 2001, a clear, sun-filled morning, I, like millions of others watched the terrorist attacks unfold on television. As usual, Rick had already called me earlier that morning to say "I love you." Shortly after the second plane hit the South Tower, he called again. Already hysterical, I picked up the phone.

"Stop crying," he said, his voice confident and calm. "I have to get all of my people out and if something happens to me, I want you to know that you made my life."

"You made my life," I responded.

I did not know it then of course, but those would be our final words. Throughout the day I talked with my daughters, his children, and many friends. Hospitals were contacted. That evening we lit candles and held a prayer vigil, but I insisted on spending the night alone. I lay on our bed, placing two pieces of his clothing next to me so I could breathe in the scent of the man I loved. I dialed his cell phone number constantly. His car was parked at the railroad station and I imagined him driving home and walking through our front door at any moment. Or maybe he was trapped in the South Tower rubble, alive, hoping a search party would find him. My half awake, dreamlike state was interrupted at around 6:00 a.m. by a call from the BBC wanting to interview me. All I remember was feeling incoherent on the phone. The rest of the week was a blur. What I do remember is being notified on Sunday, September 16, that Rick was still missing and presumed dead. When I received his death certificate in the mail, "homicide" was typed in for "cause of death."

The years since September 11, 2001, have been and continue to be hard, yet they have also given me the opportunity to connect with so many people whose lives were touched by Rick. I have also personally begun to understand the synchronicity inherent in all our lives, recognizing how events that appear unrelated often come together in meaningful ways. I believe synchronicity played a part in my decision to write this book, not just for myself, and not just as a tribute to Rick, but also for others who may come upon it and perhaps be inspired by the power that comes from living life as wholeheartedly as Rick did. To my amazement, this process has also deepened my connection to Rick, given me more time with this wonderful man, the love of my life, and ironically, helped me learn even more about him in death than I knew about him during our too short time together.

Susan Rescorla, June 2011

CHAPTER 1

Truth, Honor
and Friendship

*E*ven though I didn't think I would ever be able to handle Rick's death, he probably would have said, *"Of course you will Susan, I know what you're made of."* But we all need significant people throughout our life to support us, and for Rick, that support often came from Dan Hill and Fred McBee, his best friends. When Rick and I were married in St. Augustine, where Dan lives with his wife Pat, the only other guests were Dan and Pat's daughter Gigi, Fred, and his wife Kathy.

Like Rick, Dan was a highly decorated combat veteran, receiving the Silver Star for heroism at Trung Luong, five Bronze Stars, the Purple Heart, the Army Command medal, and the Vietnamese Cross of Gallantry with Palm Leaf. In addition to fighting in Vietnam together, Dan fought with Rick in Africa, went to Officer Candidate School the same time he did, was the best man at both of his weddings, and his children called him "Uncle Rick."

Rick met Fred while attending the University of Oklahoma. Fred was *already a student there. I think they bonded through the writing programs and their deep interest in western history. I know Rick found Fred fascinating, a westerner, a real cowboy. Fred was born in rural California, raised in the ranch country of West Texas, and rode bulls in junior rodeos. Unfortunately, Fred ruined his spinal cord when he was out just riding one of his horses. He was only 16 and has been in a wheelchair since. Fred's daughter also called Rick "Uncle Rick."*

At Morgan Stanley, Rick was worried that the World Trade Center was vulnerable to terrorist attack, and hired Dan and Fred for security consulting at various times. Fred traced flight patterns on his flight simulator software program. He determined that there was nothing to prevent someone from intentionally flying a plane into any number of highly visible structures like the Statue of Liberty, The Chrysler or Empire State Buildings, or the World Trade Center's Twin Towers. Dan helped Rick draft reports to the Port Authority recommending a number of security precautions (including moving to New Jersey), in anticipation of both the 1993 World Trade Center bombing and the 9/11 attacks.

I was on the telephone with Dan and Fred several times on 9/11. In fact, I was talking with Dan at the moment that the South Tower collapsed. Both men serve on the board of the Richard C. Rescorla Memorial, and are close and supportive friends.

DAN HILL

Rick and I had a lot of serious moments solving the problems of the world, saying if we were emperors or kings we'd square all this shit away. When it came to serious stuff, life and death, it was dead serious. But he also had this great sense of humor, and most of the time we were laughing about our former lives together. He saw a very joyful future. To Rick, it was about family, friends, good food, a couple of drinks — laughter, dancing, singing. He would say that's the *joie de vivre*, the joy of life.

I have had only one friend in my life and that was Rick Rescorla. I don't get friends, I get acquaintances. Friendship was something Rick and I finally defined. We said if you get in a financial problem a friend goes into his bank account, mortgages his house if he has to, borrows all the money he can, and if that doesn't do it he starts holding up banks to get you money. If you are under attack and think you're going to die, a friend says hang on, it's going to take me this much time to get there, but hang on, we'll die together and we'll make those sons of bitches pay for it.

Rescorla actually did that for me in Vietnam. I had about 150 men and there were 1,500 guys after us. We fought our way back to a hill, held them off, but we were running low on ammunition, and couldn't get any air support. Rick and I had this deal to always stay in touch no matter what happened. He was about 200 miles north, and I was able to radio him and told him I think it's about over, I don't think we'll make it to daylight. I said Rick, I want you to do one thing for me, keep an eye on my wife and kids, make sure they're set up. He said where you at, what coordinates, and he said hang on, I'll be there. He ordered his private to get some troops and talked to his brigade commander about more reinforcements for us. And somehow, we got out of it. He used to always say no guts no glory Hill, go out in blaze of glory, don't die an old man, and he meant it.

21

Rick was a generous man. My father was dying in 1982, a few weeks to live and I was broke at the time. I called Rick. He said I don't know how much I got but I'll send it to you and he sent me $1,500, everything he had in the bank. He said I'll see what I can borrow and send it to you even though the $1,500 was enough to do it really. He called me back later and said hey I got another $6,000. I'll wire it to you. I said don't do that Rick I don't need it, and I'll get you the $1,500 back as soon as I could. He said fuck the $1,500, it's not a loan, it's a gift, he didn't want the money back. Eventually I did a couple of jobs for him, but regardless, he was gracious enough to never mention it.

But that's just who he was, he carried his people. When Rick was in security at Morgan Stanley, he wanted his people to wear suits and look good. Many of his security guards were hurting financially. He used to pull money out of his own pocket for every son of a gun that worked for him, 40 or 50 people. He would take them in a taxicab to the garment district, get them a couple suits, shirts, ties, shoes, the works. When he noticed people doing a good job on something, he would pull a $100 bill out of his pocket and say hey, take your wife to dinner tonight. If someone needed money for prescription drugs, he'd make sure they got what they needed. If someone was going to lose their car because they were behind on payments and he heard about it, problem solved. Rick was their benefactor. He paid the hospital bills for someone's daughter who got pregnant. He supported the baby after and would say it was his grandchild. I don't know how many thousands of dollars this guy pulled out of his own pocket to do things like that.

Rick helped me with my son, who has since passed away. Rick said, "Danny's got his education, and he's always seemed pretty sharp to me, send him up, he might be good in security, let me check him out."

22

I sent the boy out to him at the World Trade Center. Rick showed him the layout and said look, I can start you out at this much, teach you daily, you come into my office each day for an hour or two, so when I retire you'll be good enough to take over my position. But the kid did not like New York City. He said he wanted to go back to St. Augustine to run a computer operation, because his family and friends were all there. Rick says Danny, you're going to make maybe one-third down there compared to what you can make here. Danny said yeah, but he wanted to be with friends and family, that was enough. Rick said, well you're a smart man, piss on the money, have a good life. Rick said he wished he could have kept him, he would have been a great asset, but he's a guy you can't buy. In fact, he said he's sort of like you Dan, he can't be bought, but unfortunately, you can be rented for relatively short periods of time.

I have never met anyone like Rick Rescorla. The man had a tremendous intellect and when he zeroed in on something he pounded it to death. Hell, he read the entire goddamn 51-volume anthology of Harvard Classics. And he didn't just read, he studied. That son of a gun could quote Shakespeare, Roman emperors, speeches by Winston Churchill. Knowing him had a tremendous impact on me because then I got into literature, writing, art, all because of his influence. I found myself thinking grander, in broader terms because Rick had a worldview.

On top of that, he was big into psychology. He studied deeply and could read people. He knew how to develop a relationship with someone and get anything he wanted out of them. He knew in a very short time all about them, their education level, what their interests were, what their big motivation in life was, and how to turn them on and off.

We were talking once after he left the military and I was still involved.

He said why are you still doing this Dan, and I said I don't know. I started doing it when I was 15 and I can't stop, probably because I'm never happier, I never feel more alive than when I'm close to death. He said ah, your *raison d'être*. I said what the fuck is your *raison d'être*, and he said it's your reason to be, and your reason to be is to lead men, to conquer giants, to overcome great enemies, to persevere, to endure. He was right, and I would use him many times to help me when I needed to know what was in somebody's head. I'd have the guy over for a few drinks with Rick, have a meal together. Later I would get back together with Rick and say, "OK, tell me about him," and he would lay it out and he would be dead on center.

Rick's intellect combined with the intelligence network he had within the United States and around the world is why he was able to predict so many things. He had contacts in government, the CIA, the FBI, different security agencies all talking to him and Rick would analyze the information and put it all together. That is why he was worried about the World Trade Center getting hit with a terrorist attack three years before the 1993 garage bombing, and how he was able to come up with the deal that the next one was going to be an air attack.

Rick had a broader perspective than anyone. Boundaries did not exist in his mind. It was relationships that mattered, and he knew his history explicitly. He knew that history repeats itself over and over and over again, and could cite a million and one examples. He told me the United States was screwing up just like the Roman Empire did years ago with our deficits. He said our national debt, when Jimmy Carter left office was over $800 billion, when Reagan left eight years later, it was $3 trillion or so, then $5 trillion after Bush, and he said this was a debt we just can't pay. The only way we're carrying it is we're borrowing and printing money. He said in the Roman Empire, an emperor came up with the idea to start diluting their money, cut it in half, and he said hell, that's what we're doing. But when the money was cut in half and the merchants found out, they started demanding two, three times as much for the same goods, and we're doing the same goddamn thing. He said they are enslaving the American public and we're going to become a nation of fucking serfs. He was talking about the problems of outsourcing years ago. It wasn't that he had a crystal ball or anything, it was just pure economic analysis, watching the trends and seeing where they were going.

On 9/11, he called me, as soon as that plane hit the North Tower. He asked me what did I think. I said back in 1947 or '48 a B-52 flew into the Empire State Building, but there was heavy fog and the navigational equipment is a thousand times better now than it was then. From what I see on TV, it's crystal clear outside so the only way to hit that goddamn tower with a 747 is if you want to. I said I think it's a hit, and he said he did to. I asked him if he was evacuating his people and he said the dumb sons of bitches from the World Trade Center said it was an accident, no problem, everyone is safe, stay at your desk. But Rick said screw it and started his evacuation plan which of course he had been working on for years. He was smart because 45 minutes later, 20 minutes later, something like that, they hit his South Tower and by then he had 70 percent of his people out of the building and the others on the stairwell on the way out. And they all did get out. He went back to do a final sweep and the South Tower collapsed, but it couldn't have been any other way because Rescorla was the kind of guy that could not quit. He knew that on the floors above him there were a lot of people trapped and he was going up to try and save them. Rick was a man that could never live with himself in the future if he did not try to save those few that were left. So he went up, the tower came down, and Rescorla is no more.

Rick often said if we don't stop our arrogant, cavalier treatment of these people we were going to pay dearly because the world has changed. It is no longer a case of great powers standing up to each other. We live in a world where four or five men secluded somewhere can make devastating strikes on us and we will never know we existed. We will have no recourse after the event because we will all be dead. These people don't just say platitudes like I'm willing to give my life — they do it. They are ready, willing and able, have done it before, do it every day, and will do it again in ever, ever and ever increasing numbers.

In fact, Rick came to my mind when that Times Square bomber was sentenced. That guy made a very prolific statement. He said, "I am but a drop in the coming flood." Now, that guy, he didn't really know how to pull a bombing off, but his philosophy, his psychology, his motivation is what is the goddamn secret to this. Most of these people we have trouble with are not idiots, they are highly educated young men under 30 with bachelors or masters degrees in the sciences, and willing to die at the snap of a finger.

Look at the 19 guys running the attack who died on 9/11. Put yourself in their spot. If you got balls big enough to take an airplane, to spend all the time it takes to learn how to fly the goddamn thing and everything else, cut throats and all this shit with box cutters, and fly the plane into a building knowing you are going to die, that takes balls bigger than goddamn bowling balls, You have to be dedicated, you have to be a true believer to do that stuff.

I don't have those kinds of balls but Rescorla did. Rescorla for Christ sake, after saving 2,700 people went back upstairs thinking he would fight through three or four more flights of stairs, through the goddamn flames, and disaster, and save all the people trapped above. Rescorla often said Dan, we're both the same. Bull shit. We weren't the same, we're not the same. I would have gotten my ass out of that building so quick I would have been kicking old ladies in wheelchairs out of my way. But Rescorla, he saved all his people and went back in to try and save the rest.

We spoke at 3:30 every afternoon. There was no decision either one of us ever made without the advice or counsel of the other. I used him as a sounding board for any philosophy, anything I was thinking about, any of my thoughts, and I don't have that now. I miss his presence, his company, his counsel. I've got to go on my own and I'm a very stupid man without Rick's guidance, less than half of what I was. It's a funny thing. Our lives became so intertwined. There was a central consciousness, we weren't any longer individuals, we became a combined, a unified mentality. He became half of me and when he died I lost half of me. There is nobody to take that place.

I've got nobody I can really tell the truth to. I have to be politically correct all the time, not offend people. You could not offend Rick. You could say anything you want and he would consider it as an idea, a concept. He would look at it, point out the advantages, the disadvantages, the positives, the negatives. Then he would say I should or shouldn't do something, or modify it in some way. And I'd do the same for him. I lost half my heart when he died. Half my mind. I'm half the man I was before Rick Rescorla died.

I miss being able to talk with him, hear his voice, reconstructing all the years we spent together and the million and one endeavors, disasters

27

and everything else we went through. He reaffirmed my life. He always encouraged me to carry on. Always. He felt there was still more to come, bigger, better things ahead of us, more than anything we had ever done before. There was always his optimism that made me believe, and when I believed, I did more, and I prospered from it.

I realized he was a special man the first few days after I met him, the way he talked, the subjects he went into, the enlightenment he brought to me about a whole bunch of things. He had a broader view of the world than I had, he expanded my world, and I started thinking on a far broader scale and continued to after that.

The play, the *Man of La Mancha*, we went to see the road show in Columbus, Georgia and later on we saw the movie. One of Rick's favorite songs, when we got a little too much to drink he used to come with that " . . . one man, scorned and covered with scars, still strove, with his last ounce of courage, to reach the unreachable stars . . ."

He died the *Man of La Mancha*, he was trying to reach an impossible star, trying to do things beyond human possibility. But he lived his whole life that way. Jesus Christ, if you read about the Ia Drang Valley, this goddamn idiot gets off the helicopters with this little platoon, goes into a battle where they are all going be slaughtered, couple hundred of his guys against thousands of them, and he tells his men, "Oh good, good, we're going to wipe them out now." And that fuckin' idiot, the amazing thing was he did it, he did it. He's got kids pissing their pants at night in foxholes and Rescorla's singing *Men of Harlech*, walking from foxhole to foxhole, encouraging them, telling them what to do, how they are going to kick the shit out of these assholes.

A normal man, the average man would be saying we're all going to fucking die tonight, and he would be in his own foxhole crying and praying for God to accept him. But Rescorla's out there saying we're gonna kick the shit out of thousands of men. People would say it was an impossible dream, but the fucker did it.

I've never regretted Rick's death. In fact, I celebrate it. Rick went out of this world the way he lived his life, flaming, bloody, a goddamn unquestionable hero, giving himself up for other people. I'd much rather see Rick Rescorla die the way he did than become an old man sitting in a corner in a chair with cancer, people feeding him.

In fact, I envy him a bit. He said we would both go out in a blaze of glory. He got a chance to do it, but it doesn't look like I'm going to. Not me, I'm going to die a silly ass old man. At 72, I've already had two heart attacks and bladder cancer. I got a little maudlin, tears started coming out talking to Jane Pauley about Rick on *Dateline NBC*. She asked is this the first time you cried, and I said yeah it is, and she said, why this long afterwards? I said I had been too proud of him, too busy cheering. I cheer his death. Rescorla would be or is thrilled with the way he died. I wish I could die like that but I ain't got the guts to do it.

FRED MCBEE

I had a 33-year long conversation with Rick. We talked almost every day, and we talked about everything.

He had a deep center. Over the years, I came to suspect that he was a man of destiny, and given the dimensions of his heroic life, I think I was right. I remember the first time I saw that iconic picture of him at the Ia Drang. We were in his front yard throwing knives and ninja stars

29

when he brought out a copy of the *US News & World Report* — the one with this stunning photograph. I had a feeling that this image would come back to haunt us. That feeling surfaced again with his picture on the cover of *We Were Soldiers Once . . . and Young*. I don't know if it was because he was born in England or what, but if you were a superstitious guy you would wonder if he was related to King Arthur. After all, he was born and raised within a stone's throw of Tintagel Castle, Arthur's home. I suppose some of it came from the culture he grew up in, some of it was genetics. However he came to be, Rick lived his life like a knight of old. He adhered to a knightly code of honor and conduct. Hell — he even slew dragons and saved damsels in distress.

Rick would never overlook an opportunity to make a generous gesture. He knew all people were human beings and he treated them that way. He treated everybody with dignity. He was pure enough to sit at Arthur's table. I'm surprised the British never knighted him. They made knights of Elton John, Paul McCartney, and not to denigrate them, but, here you got a guy, Rescorla, who was the actual embodiment of a knight. That makes me grumpy. Rick was the real thing. He was authentic, always pursuing personal excellence. To me, he was a man who soared with the eagles. He was the best single individual man I ever met or ever heard of.

I met Rick at the University of Oklahoma in the fall of 1968. I met Jim Morris at the same time. We all ended up sitting together at a table in the cafeteria. To look at that table, you'd think there must have been a terrible car wreck. Everybody sitting there was shot up or busted up in some way. I was one of two guys in wheelchairs. Another guy had an eye patch . . . another was using a cane. Must have been eight or 10 guys fresh home from Vietnam. Most of them had new pink bullet or shrapnel scars somewhere on their body. Morris had a big purple scar on his right forearm, and the fingers on that hand were floppy like wet spaghetti. He was home after his fourth tour and fifth or sixth Purple Heart. He got his last wound, the one that retired him, during the Tet offensive. I remember exactly how the introductions went:

"Jim Morris, Fifth Special Forces."

"Rick Rescorla, Seventh Cavalry."

"Ronnie Beets, 101st."

"Fred McBee, RCA."

"What?"

"Rodeo Cowboys Association."

Rick and Jim and I hit it off with each other. They were both already admitted to the Professional Writing program at Okalahoma University — a highly regarded program whose 35 students sold more books and articles than every other creative writing school in America combined. Jim had already been writing for years and had been published in magazines like *Esquire*, which pointed to him as a new Hemingway. He was working on two or three novels and a nonfiction book, but they had not been published yet.

Eventually, after a few months of heavy drinking and playing together, they convinced me to get into writing too. I wrote a shoot-em-up article called *Zip Wyatt — Winchester For Killing*. And I sold it to *Great West* magazine. On that basis, I was admitted to the writing program. Aside from my marriage to Kathy, this was the most enriching experience of my life. We weren't just students, we were writers. We swaggered around campus. We studied at the feet of great men like Dwight Swain and Foster-Harris. We were nurtured in the literary fold of authors, playwrights, editors, scholars, and other bright lights. We were getting published, something every professor at every university just wishes he could do. We felt special.

The war was still going on during those years. Hippies were doing their hippie thing. To the men at my table, the nightly news was not a political abstraction. It was very real, and we had very real friends who were still in combat. Rick and I didn't like the hippies much, but Morris, being an unconventional specialist, made friends with the long-haired rascals. He had nothing against free love.

Rick not only went to school, he almost always had two or three jobs on the side. One of them was as a Captain in the Oklahoma National Guard. He taught at the OCS Academy there. He worked the night shift as an orderly at the Oklahoma state mental hospital where he wrestled homicidal maniacs into bed every night. He traveled the state working for the Federal Law Enforcement Administration, coordinating with County Sheriffs, and signing off on machine gun acquisitions for local law enforcement.

I remember that one day a job opening was announced in the University of Oklahoma school newspaper. The U.S. Postal System had an educational subsidiary on campus, and they were advertising for martial arts experts to train U.S. postal marshals. Rick applied for the job. During his interview, the personnel manager noted Rescorla's extensive military experience, but pointed out that he did not have a black belt in any particular martial art. Several other applicants did have black belts. Rick offered to resolve the problem in typical Rescorla fashion. "May I suggest that you throw us all in a bear pit . . . and the last man standing gets the job." Rick got the job.

Rick was always busy. I swear the man never slept. But somehow we managed to spend a lot of time together. Almost every evening he would come to my house with a load of donuts and we would continue our magnificent conversation. Like I said, our conversation lasted 33 years — and damn! I wish it had lasted another 33.

The tragedy of 9/11 is that so many people knew it was coming in its general details. That's an odd feeling. Rick did, I did, Dan Hill did. It wasn't even a surprise when it happened. Rick turned in a report about it. A little proper law enforcement would have stopped it. They even had the name of one of the guys who was involved. Plenty of people knew but no one at a political level cared. Rick asked me about the possibility of a plane hitting the World Trade Center and I ran the pattern through my flight simulator software. It was clear that it would be a piece of cake. They could hit the Empire State Building, the Chrysler Building. It was so simple. We talked about somebody sitting in a cave somewhere, working it out on a computer. They could buy the software too. It was not an exotic thing to come up with, and it was obvious when you saw it on a simulator how it could happen. That kind of thing can happen by accident. It happened to that baseball player who accidentially crashed into that high-rise in New York a few years ago.

I was sleeping in on September 11th when my daughter, Hadley, called to tell me to turn on the TV.

"A plane has hit the World Trade Center. Is Uncle Rick in that building?"

Rick always expected the terrorists to come back after the 1993 hit in the World Trade Center garage. When I saw what was going on, I began to actively wait for him to call. I had a good idea of the kind of chaotic situation he was in, so I didn't call him. Susan called me before the South Tower collapsed and told me she had talked with him. She told me Rick and Dan were on the phone to each other. That figures.

When the shooting started, that's the way they liked it. In my many years of knowing both men I have often chuckled because Dan would always say that Rick Rescorla was the finest soldier he'd ever seen, and Rick would always say that Dan Hill was the finest soldier he'd ever seen. I'm pretty sure they were both right.

When I saw the tower go down, I knew Rescorla was gone. It's hard to say how you feel. On the one hand, it's a terrible pain. On the other . . . well, doggone it, Rescorla went out the way he should. It was a noble death. And he was a noble man.

If you want to get to the heart of Rescorla, look to literature. You will find him in Rudyard Kipling's famous poem *If*. This is a poem about what it takes to become a man. The standards are impossible, they cannot be achieved, but anything less is not worth striving for. You can find Rescorla in Raymond Chandler's definition of a literary hero: "Down these mean streets a man must go, who is not himself mean, who is neither tarnished nor afraid." Rick and I said that line to each other all the time — *down these mean streets, a man must go*. It was a kind of buzzword between us, indicating that we had to screw up our resolve to face the next duty before us. You will find Rescorla in Shakespeare, you will find him in Hemingway, you will find him in Homer, you will find him in Proust and Frost, and you will find him in the *Bible*.

"Greater love hath no man than this, that a man lay down his life for his friends." — (John 15:13)

CHAPTER 2

The Pride
of Cornwall

*M*y *husband was born Cyril Richard Rescorla in 1939 and raised in Hayle, Cornwall, a seaside town located at the southwest tip of England and bounded to the north by the Celtic Sea, with a three-mile coastline of sandy, picturesque beaches. During World War II, some American soldiers set up headquarters in Hayle in preparation for the invasion of Normandy. Just a little boy then, seeing the soldiers in action had a tremendous influence on Rick, and his fascination with the military led him to embark on a path that would take him all over the world.*

After enlisting in the British Army in 1957, Rick's attraction to military life led him to a recruiting office in New York's Times Square. Captivated by the energy and freedom he felt, he enlisted in the United States Army in 1963, and became an American citizen in 1967. But in his heart, Rick never really left Cornwall. He was so proud of his Cornish heritage, and Cornwall is a place I am thrilled to visit each year.

Every time I visit I go to a favorite place of ours, the Barbara Hepworth Museum and Sculpture Garden. It's up on a hilly street. You go in and there is an entranceway, bookshop, and pieces of her work. What struck me was Barbara's face seemed sculpted as beautifully as her sculptures. You walk into her gardens and she has such unusual pieces. Every piece had some kind of oval, hollowed out piece, so if you had them all lined up you would see into the ocean, which is incredible. I have become enthralled with her work and purchased many of her books. The daughter and son-in-law of our friends, Jan and Mervyn Sullivan, knew how much I loved this woman's work and surprised me with a beautiful perfume bottle with a cutout oval. Another time, I bought a beautiful moss colored vase with a hollowed out section that reminds me of her sculpture that is gorgeous.

The Cornish people have embraced Rick's memory, continued to embrace me, and let me know by word and deed, that they loved Rick as much as he loved them. That love and support began early in Rick's life. Rick was raised in a modest, working class family in Hayle. When he joined the British Army in 1957, he wrote home requesting his birth certificate. He received the birth certificate with a letter from his mother, explaining why "unknown" was written on the line for his father's name. The letter explained that his mother, and father, were actually the parents of his sister, and his sister was his real mother. The parents had raised Rick to avoid the family the scandal of having an illegitimate child. Some people in Hayle were aware of the circumstances, yet everyone held the information tightly. Rick wrote back that he was not upset, and did not consider the revelation a major issue. His attitude was he felt loved while growing up, and that was all that mattered.

Rick maintained his connections with family and friends in Cornwall and visited frequently. When the news of his role in 9/11 surfaced, it spread quickly. His singing during the evacuation of the South Tower of not only God Bless America, *but also Cornish songs, including* Men of Cornwall, *added to the pride of his countrymen. Mervyn Sullivan, Rick's childhood friend, was not surprised to learn of Rick's singing in the midst of the attacks:*

The Cornish will, as they say, *Strike Up* and start singing at any excuse to do so.

There is a tremendously close comradeship amongst us. We feel our homeland of Cornwall is a separate nation, and by joining together in song this bond is made even stronger. It's a kind of unique rebelliousness and sends out a warning that we will not be put down by any would-be challenger. This expresses itself in any situation, whether it's a time of joy or celebration and especially at a time of trouble and grief. It is a way of self-motivation and summing up courage for the challenge ahead. So, as a Cornishman, I fully understand why Rick broke into song to encourage and lead his troops in Vietnam and again when he was stimulated to lead on 9/11. Singing . . . it was a deep inbred emotion coming to the fore . . . *Onen hag Oll* (for one and all.)

On September 14, 2001, Matthew Taylor, a Member of Parliament, wrote then Prime Minister Tony Blair, nominating Rick for a posthumous bravery award. Local councillors named a sheltered housing block after him. A memorial service, held in Hayle, was attended by

37

hundreds of locals, members of Royal Air Force St. Mawgan, United States military personnel, and a Morgan Stanley representative. Family friend Aaron Sullivan was quoted by the BBC News, describing Rick as someone who "loved Cornwall and loved Hayle. He was a true Cornishman."

Within a few months, The Ballad of Rick Rescorla was written and recorded by Penzance country singer Russ Holland. The Cornish Stannary Parliament honored Rick by presenting me with The White Cross of Cornwall. The cross was made from pure Cornish tin embedded in Cornish Delabole slate in a hand-made presentation box of Cornish elm. Its etching reads "Long live Rick Rescorla" and describes him as their King Arthur.

Cornishman David Prowse wrote a beautiful poem Hero, *published in the* Cornwall Western Morning News, *about the man some called Tammy in his early years, a nickname Rick picked up for being a fan of the Bronx, New York boxer Tami Mauriello.*

HERO

A little clutch of veterans share a table in a bar,
There's a guy off in the corner coaxing tunes from his guitar.
They watch the Hudson River as it rolls towards the bend
And they talk of Rick Rescorla as a comrade and a friend.

While out across the water, many ocean-miles away
Within a Cornish Tavern by a sandy Cornish Bay,
Another group are gathered, reminiscing as a clan,
And their thoughts are all of Tammy, from the schoolboy to the man.
And every head among them has a picture in its mind

Which time and place and memory have captured and consigned,
Now the pictures weld together until only one remains,
Of a sturdy, selfless hero guiding others from the flames.

It's a picture which unites them in their glory and their grief,
More eloquent than eulogies, confirming their belief
That theirs had been a privilege to saunter at his side
And in the way he'd lived his life had Rick Rescorla died.

The veterans recalled him in the killing fields of war
As a man whose potent presence would inspire and reassure,
Just one among his brothers when the skies began to fall,
Yet one whom they regarded as a father to them all.

And now their eyes will moisten at the mention of his name
And the sources and the substance of the legend he became,
When mayhem drove the best of men to crave their mother's love,
He'd stand and croon an anthem to the gory gods above.

And on that evil morning, so deceptively serene,
Amid another carnage, just as callous and obscene
Again he took the mantle of the sainted and the strong
To save the lives of others with a blessing and a song.

Between the Hudson River and the sandy shores of Hayle,
Though eyes encompass differences of latitude and scale,
All hands are linked together in the testament they bear,
They are but Rick Rescorla's friends, united by a prayer.

39

On the first anniversary of 9/11, a magnificent six-foot stone monument, funded by donations from people throughout Cornwall, was unveiled in Rick's honor in Hayle. The plaque on the monument reads:

**Cyril Richard "Rick" Rescorla
Hayle 1939-2001 New York
Rick Gave His Life In The Terrorist Attack
On The World Trade Center, New York
September 11th, 2001. While Directing The Evacuation,
His Actions On The Day Saved Over 2,700 Lives.
"Greater Love Hath No Man."**

Former Hayle Councillor Bob Butler said of the monument: "This is the sort of thing that's going to be here long after I and the majority of the young people in the town have gone. In years to come, people will say 'what was all that about,' and obviously they will be told. They will remember him in the future as we remember him now — for the heroism that occurred on that day by him."

Rick's cousin Jon was involved in the fundraising for the beautiful monument, which included an eagle in flight on top of it. Jon surprised me by ordering another eagle and mailed it to me. The eagle arrived in a huge, heavy box. It was placed in my kitchen, and will be with me wherever I may live. The monument was placed at the waters edge in Hayle, across from where Rick was born. Surrounded by beautiful gardens, the location is near where he and his grandfather would go out in their rowboat, and I know the setting would have great meaning to Rick.

There were enough funds left to create the "Rick Rescorla Wildlife Garden," at the Penpol Primary School that Rick attended as a child. The garden serves as a meditative area at times, and is filled with tiny ponds, frogs and a butterfly area with butterfly bushes. There are birds nests, a hollowed out tree, and an area where children can sit on a hilltop while their teacher reads to them. The students have cameras on their computers so they can visit the garden from their desks. Paul Hodson, Head Teacher at Penpol School, described the impact Rick continues having on his students.

PAUL HODSON

The Penpol School currently has over 300 pupils and we are very proud of the fact that we are classified as an "outstanding" school by government inspectors due to the wonderful progress made by our children. Our mission is to help every single child that passes through our school to be brave and attempt everything offered to them in the hope that they will find something in life that they love and become happy, helpful citizens.

A number of Penpol graduates became heroes and we celebrate our heroes in assemblies and in our curriculum. We have Penpol heroes who battle against terrible illnesses and still dedicate their lives to helping others. We have a hero who, as a young man, dreamed of climbing to the top of Everest. On his final attempt, with the summit in reach, he saw a dying man with a shattered leg. Without hesitation he gave up his dream and risked his own life to rescue the man who survived after a twenty-hour descent.

Rick Rescorla is our greatest hero. Each year we hold a special assembly to tell his incredible story and inspire our pupils. Rick attended Penpol during the war and was clearly a top student, winning a scholarship and a place on the school Honours List in 1950. At that time the school was small, just a few rooms and outdoor assemblies when the weather was dry. The boys were given the task of loading coal into the boiler during winter and the subjects were typical of the time. Teachers were strict, but the school was and still is a very happy place. Rick loved to run down to the harbour to watch the American soldiers who were preparing for the Normandy landings. One day they were all gone.

We are so grateful to Susan for helping us construct a wonderful living memorial, which is called the Rick Rescorla Wildlife Garden. This is the favourite place for most people in the school. We learn in the garden, play music and create art there. We also use it as a special place where people can find peace. If a child is feeling sad or angry a staff member will walk around the beautiful garden and the magic of the place brings healing.

We will never forget Rick. He is our hero, our role model. I am sure that Rick would appreciate our school motto, "Forward Together." We are all in this world together and we need to move through our trials and tribulations together, with someone like Rick leading the way!

I am also extremely grateful to representatives of the UK who have been so wonderful in always counting me as one of them, even though Rick lived in America for a very long time. I have been informed of everything going on with respect to honoring the 80 UK victims of 9/11. I received an invitation from Princess Anne to attend a memorial service she was having at London's Grosvenor Square. I was unable to attend but asked Rick's brother Clive if he could represent the family, which he did.

I somehow managed to travel to the UK on my own, not long after 9/11. I received an invitation from Prince Charles, who was honoring those who lost someone with UK roots. Still disoriented, shocked, and now wheelchair bound on orders from my doctor as a result of high blood pressure, I was determined to attend and I did. I went with Jon, and we both found Prince Charles to be extremely gracious as he took time to speak either individually or in small groups with everyone. We also toured his lovely gardens, which he said he spent a great deal of time working on.

Heart of a Soldier *had been published by then, and before leaving I gave Prince Charles a copy and said: "My husband was a Cornishman and after all, you are the Duke of Cornwall."*

I do not know if he ever read the book, but it was very meaningful to me to be able to present it to him.

MERVYN SULLIVAN

Mervyn Sullivan was one of Rick's best friends growing up. I first met Mervyn and his wife Jan when Rick and I went to Cornwall for our honeymoon. I spend time with them every year when I visit Cornwall and they are both among my closest friends. A meter reader for the electricity board, Mervyn has become a wonderful painter during his retirement and gave us a beautiful abstract landscape of the river Hayle for a wedding gift.

I first met Rick during the Second World War, when I was about four years old, but then I knew him as Cyril, the name his mother wanted him called. This was a popular name given to children at that time and suited this fairfaced curly haired boy. My mother and Rick's grandfather both worked at the local electricity generating station in our hometown of Hayle, a small but very busy industrial port on the north coast of Cornwall, the most south westerly county in Great Britain. Both Rick and I used to wait at the front gate of the power station for our "parents" to leave work and we would walk home with them.

We were also good friends when we attended Penpol School at our end of the town. This friendship continued when we both went to the Penzance Grammar School, some eight miles away from Hayle. To get there we used to travel by steam train. There were some eight to 10 pupils traveling by train to the same school and Rick took it on his own back to organize us by becoming the self-appointed "leader" of the students on the train. With his large physique and commanding voice it seemed natural for us to accept his leading role. If the train was late he would form us up as a unit and he would take the lead and run us for half a mile uphill to the school and he would report to the headmaster as to why we were late. And his explanation was always accepted!

We played for the same local rugby football team and to this day I have a constant reminder of Rick in the form of stitches on my forehead where he unwittingly kicked me when we were both playing on the same side! We stayed good friends up until the time we went our different ways at about the age of eighteen. For all of our middle stages of our lives I never saw Rick, but I was kept informed of Rick by his mother Cissy who lived in Hayle all of her life, as I did.

In his later life Rick would come back to Cornwall from the USA to see his mother as often as he could and we would meet up. He would always call on his relatives and old friends of his family. He loved his native homeland and would tour Cornwall immersing himself in the culture and history of his Cornish motherland. We would reminisce about the old days and he would want to know all about the friends he had when he was living in Hayle.

In the early mornings, after he ate a hearty breakfast in a local cafe, we would walk on the cliffs above the local beach. Rick reveled in the silence, the absence of people, the spaciousness and splendour of the view over the blue ocean. He would often say how much he envied me living just five minutes from this, in his words "absolute paradise." The reason being that this was a million miles from his high-powered lifestyle in America. Overlooking the sea he would close his eyes and faultlessly quote lengthy passages of prose and poems by famous writers and poets. The most telling and powerful of these being the battle speech from Henry V by William Shakespeare. By quoting this I felt that Rick was inspiring himself to face up to whatever life was to throw at him in the future. Rick was also very knowledgeable about art and pottery and was indeed a very accomplished potter. He confided in me that when he retired he would use much of his retirement years making pottery.

When Rick brought Susan over to Cornwall, my wife Jan and I met up with them and we would visit interesting historic churches and places of local interest. Rick wanted to tell and show Susan as much as he could of his fascinating birthplace. Rick was so knowledgeable about Cornwall that he even amazed me, a local who had never left the area. This knowledge was acquired by reading countless Cornish books over the years. As my son Aaron put it, Rick was someone "who loved Cornwall, and he loved Hayle. He was always thinking of Cornwall and he was a true Cornishman."

Rick was an amazing man who had the unique capability of making you feel so good about yourself. After speaking with him you felt that you had been put on a pedestal. Anyone who ever met Rick will tell you that they will never forget the experience. I have never met anyone who could come anywhere near to Rick as being a true human being.

CHAPTER 3

A Legacy
of Courage

"Father God, whose Son told us that greater love hath no man that he lay down his life for his friend, we call upon you to be with us in this gathering, this memory place, to remember the many who gave their life for others, and especially, we ask thy blessing upon this occasion, where we remember a gallant man, a gallant soldier, a gallant citizen who also gave the full measure of devotion for others."

Chaplain Bill Lord's invocation at the dedication of Rick's statue at Fort Benning.

*F*red McBee first thought of having a statue built to honor Rick. *I had been asked to accept the New Jersey Vietnam Service Medal, which was being posthumously awarded to Rick at a ceremony on May 7, 2002, at the New Jersey Vietnam Veterans' Memorial in Holmdel, New Jersey, located on the grounds of the PNC Bank Arts Center. General Hal Moore was the featured speaker, and during his*

47

remarks he happened to mention how statues had been built to honor lesser men than Rick, and it apparently hit Fred that we needed a statue to honor Rick. As the concept evolved, there was never any question that Fort Benning was the best home for Rick's statue. Fort Benning was where Rick attended Officer Candidate School (OCS), where he trained and left for Vietnam, and where, in April 2001, he was inducted into the OCS Hall of Fame.

There was a fair amount of red tape involved in being granted permission to have the statue — the only one I think done of anyone killed on 9/11 — placed at a military site, which I suppose was understandable. Yet, despite the complications and predictable bureaucracy, the people of Fort Benning did a fantastic job.

Edward Hlavka, who lived in Utah at the time, sculpted the bronze statue. While doing research on sculptors, Fred came across Ed's work. After speaking with him by phone, Fred believed that Ed "really got Rick," and would likely do a good job. Fred was right. From the start, Ed immersed himself in the project. His sculpture was based on Rick's picture from the We Were Soldiers Once . . . and Young *cover, but Ed still wanted to come as close to knowing Rick as possible. I think he studied Rick at virtually every age of his life, spoke with Dan, Fred, and I, asked for pieces of Rick's clothing to hold, examined his medals, his dog tags, and even got some elephant grass from Vietnam. He wanted to feel Rick, the man, and get into his head. Ed did a fantastic job and he was also kind enough to send me a bust he made of how Rick looked in 2001, the Rick that I really knew. I keep the bust in my office and it is a beautiful piece.*

Raising funds for the sculpture was difficult and time consuming, but with the help of Dan, Fred, and many others, we were successful.

Our campaign was kicked off with a $25,000 donation from Morgan Stanley, and we held Heart of a Soldier *book signings at a Morgan Stanley office in Virginia, and one in Pennsylvania. Additionally, Nick Snider did a wonderful job organizing a book signing at the National Museum of Patriotism in Atlanta. We also held a golf outing and received many donations from people online and somehow raised the $100,000 needed to commission the piece.*

The unveiling took place on April 1, 2006. I wanted everyone from the military represented together as equals to honor not only Rick, but our great country as well. I invited Medal of Honor recipients, OCS officers, and of course, members of the Seventh Calvary. Some people just showed up, including a nurse from California who had been in Vietnam during that time. I was very excited that Sergeant Artie Muller, a Vietnam veteran and the National Executive Director of The Rolling Thunder, a group that raises awareness of Missing in Action and Prisoner of War soldiers, could be a speaker. There were other military veteran's groups that rode down by motorcycle.

It was tremendous bringing approximately 500 people together. However, at the time, it was hard to predict how many people would make the trip. I told a reporter that I estimated about 80 or 100 people, but we ended up with a great turnout. When I think back to that day, the best part was that everyone was represented, everyone was equal, and all of us were united.

There were however, some tense moments the night before the ceremony because the statue had still not arrived. It was touch and go and I think it was around 10:30 or 11:00 p.m. when it finally arrived. I was able to get a look at it by climbing up a step ladder and removing part of the covering, and I thought, "Oh my God." It was just unbelievable how

49

lifelike it looked. So the next morning, all was well. Just before the ceremony, the Rolling Thunder and several other motorcycle groups representing military veterans appeared and the tremendous roar was powerful. The ceremony began with a woman softly playing a bagpipe, which Rick would have loved, and opened with remarks by Brigadier General James Yarbrough.

BRIGADIER GENERAL JAMES YARBOROUGH

Brigadier General Yarbrough's remarks set just the right tone for the ceremony. At the time he was the Deputy Commanding General, United States Army Infantry Center, at Fort Benning. Raised in an Army family, he served in Afghanistan and Iraq, and is now a Brigadier General with many personal and unit awards and decorations.

Good morning. I know there are folks from all over the country, from all over the world here, and it is a privilege to unveil this monument of Rick Rescorla, a true soldier and American hero. I think you all recognize that this isn't a museum of interesting artifacts and displays, but it is a place where stories are told, stories of men in combat owning the last 100 meters. And we do this in front of all 50 flags knowing all 50 states stand together.

In Rick's own words, it's a great day to be an American. Rick took the lessons he learned in the army and applied them to everyday life. There is an age-old debate about whether great leaders are born naturally or are they made through development. My cut is it's a little of both. It starts with instincts, but you have to learn to act on those instincts. I don't second guess those people in the business of providing emergency response, but I'll tell you that Rick's gut probably tightened up a bit when those instructions came to remain inside. But I believe it was destiny for him to be hired there and be personally responsible for security in the towers; and destiny that he acted on instinct against recommendations and direction of those in the business of giving direction, and being personally responsible for saving the lives of 2,700 Americans. In the middle of the battle, he was stone calm, as only our greatest leaders are, surveying his surroundings. This is a great day to be an American, a great day to honor Rick Rescorla, and Susan, we're pleased you chose Fort Benning.

Then it was my turn to say a few words. When I spoke, I recognized the people there as Rick's "brothers and his heroes" and was honored to be in their company. I said the legacy we are leaving insures that no one forgets what Rick did that day and before, and that the United States will not forget what happened on 9/11, and that as a nation we must be vigilant, support our military 100 percent, and honor Rick as a new hero in a new millennium. I closed with the words that Morgan Stanley employees reported that Rick said during the evacuation on 9/11: "Today is a day to be proud to be an American, tomorrow the world will be looking at you."

MERVYN SULLIVAN

While Rick had become a true American, he never forgot his Cornish roots. So it was very special to have Rick's friend from childhood, Mervyn

Sullivan, and his wife Jan in attendance. They traveled from Cornwall, and surprised me by bringing and presenting the Cornish flag on Rick's behalf.

It is an honor to be here. The Rick you knew is the Rick in this statue. But the Rick I knew was four years old, and we were very close friends until he left Cornwall at 17. Rick was proud to fight under the American flag, but he lived his life under the Cornish flag. If Rick was here now he would wrap himself in this flag and shed tears, I guarantee it. Rick Rescorla, *Onen hag Oll!*

GENERAL HAL MOORE (RET.)

It was quite an honor to have General Moore as a speaker. While some only knew of General Moore as the co-author of We Were Soldiers Once . . . and Young, *Rick knew him as the man who commanded the 7th Cavalry at the Battle of Ia Drang Valley. Rick had shared how in the midst of battle, General Moore, with tears in his eyes, reminded his troops that they were obligated to retrieve the men who were killed on the battlefield so they could be respectfully returned to their families.*

That kind of compassion was also evident in General Moore's late wife Julia as well, who I was acquainted with. A U.S. Army daughter, wife and mother, Julia is credited with influencing the Pentagon to require an officer and a chaplain to personally deliver the news of a fallen soldier following the Battle of Ia Drang Valley, and helped to develop the "survivor support networks," which remain in use to this day.

A Legacy of Courage

I know Rick treasured the inscription General Moore wrote in his copy of We Were Soldiers Once. . . and Young, *which read:*

To Rick Rescorla,
extraordinary battlefield leader;
quite simply the best Platoon leader of Infantry
I have ever known in two wars.

With love and highest respect
Hal Moore
8 Nov '92

About 1:30 in the morning in the early morning darkness on November 15, 1965. The place, X-ray battle ground in the Ia Drang Valley of Vietnam. I was awake and alert in my 7th Cavalry command post when I heard a strange sound which I had never heard before on any battlefield in Korea or in Vietnam. A man was *singing*, in a rich baritone. Who was it? Second Lieutenant Rick Rescorla.

The previous morning another rifle company was viscously attacked by 500 of the enemy. At that very position, now occupied by Rick, they lost 62 officers, men killed or wounded. A fresh 7th Calvary company, Rick's platoon, relieved that company on the line. And now, Rick was singing slow and steady, Cornish tunes, to ease the tension of his men. Late that night the enemy had heavy loses in three separate attacks. Not one man in Rick's company was killed. Six were lightly wounded.

After that battle, I was in a lot of firefights with Rick and he was the absolute best combat platoon leader that I have served with in two wars. In the Ia Drang Valley in 1965 in X-ray Albany, Rick Rescorla became a battlefield legend in the 7th Cavalry.

53

Now I'm going to talk directly to you Rick, and I know you're here in spirit with us. Rick, we miss you. We miss your wit, your presence, your creativity, and your charismatic magnetism. But we love and respect you so much we will be with you again. And like I told you a few years ago, when each of us lifts off from this temporary holding area and are approaching our eternal objective, I want to remind you yet again Rick, pop smoke, so we can come in on the right landing zone.

SERGEANT ALLEN LYNCH (RET.)

Medal of Honor recipient Allen James Lynch followed General Moore's moving words. While we talked by telephone before the unveiling, I didn't know Sergeant Lynch, but he was suggested as a speaker to me by some of the guys from the 1st Cavalry in New Jersey. Sergeant Lynch knew Rick and served in the army from 1964-1969.

You could be in a room with 15 or 20 other people and you remember Rick of all of them, he was that kind of guy. He was always a tremendous leader and we all looked up to him, his leadership and what he stood for. I think it's kind of sad today that when you want to use the word hero it doesn't really have the meaning that it should. It seems everybody is a hero, from the guy that goes out and plays a good golf game, to a guy who runs a 50-yard dash with a football in his hand, to an actor, to some political activist that stands up for something, to some movie actor who never saw a shot fired in anger, they are all heroes. And when we really want to see that word in the classic sense of what a hero really is, that is a Rick Rescorla. That really epitomizes what heroism really is, it just doesn't seem to be enough anymore because of its total, complete misuse by so many people.

And yet, if Rick would have been born in a different era, in a different time, songs around the campfire would have been sung about him, and stories would have told about his exploits, and he would have been a hero for generations to come. I think he will be that, I think he will. And I think that we need to start taking back the word hero and challenging the use of that word. And when we do, we need to think about the Rick Rescorla's. And when we hear someone say that so and so is a hero of the gridiron, we need to say no, no, no, you don't understand. Rick Rescorla was a hero, that's what a real hero is.

PRIVATE FIRST CLASS SAM FANTINO (RET.)

Sam Fantino was Rick's radio operator in Vietnam. Rick felt Sam saved his life during the Battle of Ia Drang Valley and should have been awarded a Bronze Star. When that didn't happen, Rick gave Sam his Bronze Star during one of his visits. We stayed with Sam and his wife Lorrie in Illinois before we were married. On 9/11, Sam and I spoke several times.

C.S. Lewis said, ". . . aim at heaven and you get the earth thrown in. Aim at earth and you get neither." Rick aimed for heaven every minute every day. This extraordinary man meant so much to so many of us. Rick knew how to cut through any confusion, he knew how to unite, inspire and motivate people. His very last moments on this earth were literally spent aiming for heaven. On 9/11 he was last seen walking up the stairs of the World Trade Center in search of stragglers in the general direction of heaven.

Rick is someone who never thought twice about laying down his life for someone else. When he called Susan on 9/11, he said he was going back in and would probably not be coming home. When she asked him why he was going back, he simply said there are still people inside. He never hesitated. Rick's actions take the kind of courage that most of us will never know.

I like to think Rick is serving in the ultimate army now, and maybe that's why he was taken. The Lord simply could not bear to be without him any more, and he still has important work to do. I know in my heart I will see Rick Rescorla again, and when I do, I will recognize him by his singing.

SERGEANT ARTIE MULLER

I first learned about Artie Muller and his organization, The Rolling Thunder, from watching a news report on television of how the group held a motorcycle "Ride for Freedom" every Memorial Day, that had grown from 2,500 to an estimated 900,000 participants/spectators. The Rolling Thunder is committed to raising awareness of the thousands of POW and MIA soldiers. I have since gotten to know Artie and his wife Elaine, laugh with them, and respect his organization's unwavering commitment to our POW's and MIA's.

To all of you that served in different wars, to my brother and sister Vietnam vets, welcome home. Rick Rescorla was born in the United

Kingdom, in Cornwall, came to America, fought in one of the fiercest battles in Vietnam, became an American citizen, and went on to work as a vice president in charge of security for a major company. He warned his company, he warned the government that sooner or later, something was going to happen at the World Trade Center. He made his people participate in drills, even when they didn't want to. When something did happen, his people got out safely, but he went back in and his security people followed.

When the South Tower went down, Rick and some of them were inside. Who knows how many lives were saved that day. It is important that future generations are taught about what went on that day, and it is important that America always stands strong and stands together. It doesn't matter what color you are, what religion you are, we all eat the same way, we are all strong together. This country has the most freedom in the world and we should all be proud to wear the uniform of a soldier.

JOSEPH GALLOWAY

We were fortunate that Joe Galloway, who co-authored with General Moore, We Were Soldiers Once . . . and Young, *was able to attend the unveiling and be one of our speakers. A former* U.S. News & World Report *senior editor, Joe was in Vietnam as a military correspondent for United Press International during the Battle of Ia Drang Valley. Joe was the only civilian awarded the Bronze Star by the United States Army during the Vietnam War.*

I met Rick for the first time on Nov. 14, 1965. I met him because I'd been told they didn't have any room on the helicopters during that lift into X-ray, but I went along and I found a seat and sort of slid into it and hoped I wouldn't be noticed. Along comes a very busy lieutenant with a guy behind him and it was Rick Rescorla. And he looked in that helicopter counting heads and he said to me, "Who the hell are you?"

I said, "I am a reporter."

And he said, "Well get the hell off, I got a medic here who needs a ride."

You can't argue with that. I got off and I went to see Rick again, and again, in that battlefield and others. He was a warrior prince. And Al Lynch is right. Our society has devalued and confused the word hero. We mistake victims for heroes, and we've vastly expanded the definition of victim too. But they ain't heroes. Heroism is something else. It's doing what Rick Rescorla did. Giving of his own well of courage to his soldiers, frightened as they were at 0300 on a dark night when they know the enemy is coming for them. It is giving from his well of courage to those frightened people in a stairwell when the building rocks and shakes from the impact of the highjacked airliner and smoke starts filling that stairwell, and he sings to them. He sings *God Bless America,* and he tells them things to steady their nerves. That's a hero.

When they attacked the Trade Center and the Pentagon, I was standing in line at the badge office at the U.S. State Department. I had been sworn into service as a special consultant to General Colin Powell on September 10th. Timing is everything. So I'm standing in line at the badge office the next day and they're calling for the evacuation of the building, I'm looking at the TV and I saw what was going down and I knew, in that moment, I thought of my friend Rick Rescorla, in that

Trade Center, and I knew where he was, I knew where he had to be, and I wept for him and all the others who died there. And then we find that he saved the lives of 2,700 individuals. But for that one man the death toll on 9/11 would have been double of what it was. Now that my friends is a hero, that's our friend. Rick Rescorla.

THE DEDICATION

Following Joe's stirring words, I placed a wreath of white roses at the base of the statue. Dan and Fred removed the covering from the statue and I touched the magnificent piece with my right hand. Then Fred read the dedication to Rick that he wrote.

Second Lieutenant Rick Rescorla, Battle of Ia Drang, Vietnam 1965, Cyril Richard Rick Rescorla, was born in Hayle, Cornwall, United Kingdom, in 1939. He enlisted in the British Army and served in Cyprus and Rhodesia. In 1963 he immigrated to America, joined the United States Army, graduated from Officer Candidate School and fought heroically with the 7th Cavalry in 1965 and 1966. In 1967 he became an American citizen. In 1993 Rescorla was Vice President for Corporate Security for Dean Witter Morgan Stanley company when the World Trade Center was bombed the first time. He led the evacuation that day and stayed in the smoldering building for 12 hours, helping firefighters rescue trapped survivors. After the terrorist attack on September 11, 2001, Rescorla again led the evacuation of the World Trade Center. He was last seen going upstairs into the burning building, conducting a final sweep for survivors. He was killed when the South Tower collapsed. His actions that day saved the lives of more than 2,700. In life and in death, Rescorla epitomized the soldier's code: leave no man behind.

The ceremony concluded with the playing of Gary Owen, *the traditional Irish marching tune and the 7th Cavalry's call to arms, a seven-gun salute, and the playing of Taps. Many people lingered by the statue, paying tribute, praying silently, and taking pictures. A few days later, Joe Galloway wrote an article about the unveiling that was published on The Military.com website, a military and veteran organization with 10 million members.*

REMEMBERING A TRUE HERO
By Joe Galloway

FORT BENNING, Ga. — The word "hero" has been so debased and over-used in our modern society that it is almost meaningless when applied to the real thing.

This past week, here at the U.S. Army home of the infantry, several hundred people gathered for the dedication of a larger-than-life bronze statue of a real American hero named Rick Rescorla.

The statue is iconic: the young infantry 2nd lieutenant platoon leader leading the way in combat, his M-16 rifle with bayonet attached ready for use. It is based largely on the photograph on the cover of the book *We Were Soldiers Once . . . and Young*, written by Lt. Gen. Hal Moore and me, which tells the story of the deadly battles in the Ia Drang Valley in the dawn of the Vietnam War.

Rescorla was a hero of the battles of Landing Zone X-ray and Landing

60

Zone Albany. He earned a Silver Star, the third highest military medal for heroism, for his sterling leadership of a platoon of Bravo Company 2nd Battalion 7th U.S. Cavalry, 1st Cavalry Division (Airmobile) in those battles in November of 1965. But that statue in the home and headquarters and training ground for the mud-foot infantry was the result of unvarnished heroism long after the British-born Rescorla left the Army, became an American citizen and retired from the Army Reserve with the rank of colonel.

The statue of the young Rescorla was born out of what he did as an older, heavier civilian vice president for security for Morgan Stanley in New York City. The brokerage firm occupied 22 floors of the South Tower in the World Trade Center.

Ever since the failed terrorist truck bombing in 1993 in the basement of that building, Rescorla was convinced that the terrorists would come back to finish the job. He urged Morgan Stanley to build its own low-rise high-security headquarters across the river in New Jersey where most of its employees lived. Not possible, he was told, because the firm had a long-term lease on those 22 floors.

Rescorla fought for the time and money needed for half a dozen surprise full evacuation drills each year. And, yes, he knew how much it cost to pull a couple thousand stockbrokers off their telephones. He knew and didn't care.

On September 11, 2001, Rescorla stood at the window of his office and watched the tower across the way burn. The Port Authority Police squawk box on the wall urged everyone in the other buildings of the Trade Center to remain at their desks and not panic. You are safe, the reassuring voice said.

Rescorla responded with a curt word: "Bull — !" He grabbed his bullhorn and moved floor-by-floor ordering Morgan Stanley's 2,700 workers to evacuate immediately. They knew where to go and how to do that, thanks to Rick. Two by two, the old buddy system, they began the long walk down the stairs to the street.

Halfway down the second hijacked airliner plowed into their building. The building shook and swayed to the impact. Smoke began filling the stairwells. People were frightened. Rick Rescorla used his bullhorn again. This time he sang to the evacuees, just as he sang to his soldiers on a long night in Vietnam. He sang *God Bless America*. He sang the songs of the British Army in the Zulu Wars. He sang the old Welsh miner songs.

He got them all out and headed for safety down the streets away from the World Trade Center. Four of his own security people were still up clearing the Morgan Stanley floors so Rick Rescorla turned and headed back up the stairs with New York City firemen. None of them made it out alive and neither did Rick Rescorla.

Among those at the dedication were plenty of other real American heroes. There were three recipients of the Medal of Honor for heroism above and beyond the call of duty. Scores of veterans of America's wars of the past half-century and more. Also, General Moore and his sidekick Sgt. Maj. Basil L. Plumley.

As I sat there looking at the statue of Rick my mind carried me back 40 years to that terrible November in Vietnam and the words of the young Rescorla as he and his battle-weary soldiers strode into the surrounded position at LZ Albany to rescue their decimated battalion: "Good, Good, Good! I hope they hit us with everything they got tonight — we'll wipe them up."

You want a definition of the word hero? In my dictionary it says simply: Rick Rescorla.

CHAPTER 4

Brothers in Arms

"Many times, Rescorla cradled the bodies of his dying soldiers, speaking softly and reassuringly to them. 'You're going to be all right,' he promised, no matter how dire the situation. After a soldier died, Rescorla would cover his hands with the soldier's blood, in a sort of ritual."

From *The New Yorker* article "The Real Heroes Are Dead," By James B. Stewart

James Stewart certainly captured the intensity of Rick's Vietnam experience in The New Yorker *article and his book* Heart of a Soldier. *However, during our time together, Rick did not dwell on his time in the military, preferring to live in the present and always looking forward to life's next great adventure. But he remained close with the men he knew from the battles he fought. When visiting with someone he had served with, or talking on the phone, it was obvious how highly he regarded them, and in turn, how highly they regarded him.*

Over the years, Rick's legacy has continued to flourish. Most recently, the Forward Operating Base (FOB), in Farah Province, Afghanistan, was named FOB Rescorla. Many of Rick's Brothers In Arms were honored to have an opportunity to share their reflections and I am honored to include them.

SERGEANT JOE HOLLOWAY (RET.)

Joe Holloway (Doc) was Rick's medic in Vietnam. Joe visited our home and had dinner with us several times. Rick liked Joe very much, and Joe was a regular part of the prayer circle we held each night following 9/11. Joe and I have kept in touch and he always ends his emails with Gary Owen, *the motto of the 7th Cavalry in Vietnam.*

I was blessed to have Rick as a leader during the most dangerous time of my life. A person lives and leaves this life in a short span of time. However, what he leaves in our hearts and mind is everlasting. Rick will always be a part of me and I will share with others what he shared with me: Character that is poised and positive, intelligence, courage, conviction, self awareness, guidance from above, commitment to faith, duty, honor, discipline, determination, sensitivity, brotherhood, friendship, leadership, a quest for knowledge, for love, for happiness! This and much more he shared with those who were fortunate enough to know this noble soul and it was given as freely as a wave of the hand. Most of all to me he is my friend, a true brother who I honor.

SECOND LIEUTENANT JIM KELLY (RET.)

Patrick Kelly, who everyone calls Jim, maintained a close friendship with Rick after Vietnam. Jim has continued being a terrific friend to me. We correspond regularly and his support over the years has been remarkable. Like so many from that period, Jim is someone who has stepped into my life and made it better. Jim began his thoughts about Rick with a quote by Heraclitus, the Greek philosopher.

> "Out of every one hundred men, ten shouldn't even be there, eighty are just targets, nine are the real fighters, and we are lucky to have them, for they make the battle. Ah, but the one, one is a warrior, and he will bring the others back."

I met Rick at Fort Benning and we had great respect for each other. After the Army we lost touch (except to fill out some security forms for him in the mid 1980s.) I also received a call from him in the mid 1990s during a difficult period of my life. What a relief it was to hear from Rick at that time. Talking to him made those issues remote. I recovered from the malaise and never looked back, until 9/11.

He was a fine, no, a magnificent warrior. Those people are few and far between and we are very lucky to have those few (and most fortunate when we know one and we can count him as a friend). The warrior knows he can only do his job when he can do it without reservation and without fear. The lack of fear is only achieved when the warrior realizes he is already dead, so there is no sense in trying to save himself. The Sioux have a phrase that is used in an attempt to achieve that high mental plateau . . . Hoka Hey . . . it is a good day to die. That was my thought of Rick on 9/11 when my wife Janet spoke to you on the phone that night.

COLONEL WILLIAM FOLEY, JR. (RET.)

William Foley, Jr., Ph.D. was also in Vietnam with Rick. Bill is currently a professor at Indiana University-Purdue University Indianapolis, and specializes in Public Safety, Homeland Security and Executive Education. Bill is on a mission to make sure that is Rick posthumously awarded the Presidential Medal of Freedom, the highest civilian award you can receive. He has been a great friend to me and supportive from the beginning.

Rick was a true friend. I first met him in October 1964. We were all young then, yet Rick stood out among all of us. It was not just his Cornish accent, but rather the sense of genuine friendship and honesty he exhibited. That was in the human dimension, he genuinely cared about each of us and our concerns. I was the second youngest in my Officer Candidate School class, with only 13 months of Army experience under my belt. When I reported to Infantry OCS, Rick could have dismissed me as someone between a nuisance and a nobody — among the many great soldiers of our class. He did not. He always had time and made time to help me and answer my questions, plus freely gave good advice, and had a sense of humor as well.

We became friends and we played on some of the same flag football teams there during "time off," in this 24-week grueling experience. It was easy to recognize the true leadership dimension of Candidate

Rescorla. Leaders can be either made or born, but Rick possessed the quiet character traits which later would propel him to the top of the Army Infantry as a full Colonel and into the memory of our Nation forever. He always made sure things were OK with us on the night patrols, at the live fire ranges, in cliff rappelling, and in helicopter and armor operations — all of it dangerous. With all the attributes, traits and principles, Rick Rescorla simply put — was a great American and a really good person. He is now remembered in our American legacy, in classes here, at the Garden of Heroes of the United States Army War College, at Fort Benning, at Arlington National Cemetery and around the world. He was a good and humble man, the bravest of the brave, and is sadly missed.

SPECIALIST RONNIE GUYER (RET.)

Ronnie Guyer, who lives in California, served in Vietnam with Rick. Ronnie has continued to be a loyal, wonderful friend to me since 9/11, and he is always doing so much to raise people's awareness of Rick's story. Ronnie is currently a Field Representative for California State Assemblyman Van Thai Tran, the 1st Vietnamese-American to be sworn into a State Legislature in U.S. history. In an email with the subject "how Rick Rescorla inspired me," Ronnie wrote the following.

In the 1st Battalion, 7th U.S. 7th Cavalry Regiment, I was a Vietnam Radioman/Driver for Lt. Colonel Hal G. Moore, and his Sgt. Major Basil Plumlely, in a then free South Vietnam's Central Highlands of 1965. Early on we would hear the 2nd Battalion's Lt. Rick Rescorla sing to his men over our field radios, to inspire them while on perimeter guard duty at our 1st Cavalry Division (Airmobile) Base Camp. "An Officer singing to his men, what's he singing to his men for?" was Moore and Plumley's initial incredulous reaction.

"Well, whatever works for them," I said.

And work it did, for Rick Rescorla was even then laying the groundwork for his fellow soldiers to be all that they already are in God's eyes, especially in forthcoming combat against all odds. This was grandly proved out while we were in the fight for our lives in a Valley of Death called the Ia Drang Valley Battle in November 1965. While surrounded by overwhelming enemy, Lt. Rick Rescorla's men staved off human wave assault after human assault to victory, while Rick inspiringly sang to them as I listened on our field radios. A preview of things to come later on after the Vietnam War.

While witnessing this ferocious battle, from a nearby Artillery Support Landing Zone position, I had personally witnessed that there really is such a thing as hate in this world, and people out there who hate the free for being free! Something that defined both Rick Rescorla and myself for the rest of our lives.

Rick Rescorla carried this firsthand clarity on to new heights at New York City's World Trade Center, saving many more lives in the process in a new time of war. For the rest of my life I went on to continue supporting our hero soldiers fighting on behalf of the freedom of others, and their loved ones who wait for them to come home or not. I've also dedicated my life to help people clearly see just how our own freedom is at risk and thus must be protected ever vigilantly. As Rick Rescorla always did.

Ever since that Valley of Death long ago, we also came to see that

Love is indeed the only reality, not hate. And further, that Love only comes when people are free!

Rick Rescorla loved us all very, very much. In doing so he selflessly sacrificed all that he was on behalf of others, setting the most loving of examples for the rest of us to follow, both personally and professionally. In loving his now 9/11 widow Susan so very deeply, Rick showed us exactly where the true happiness in life is. It is in our sacrificing, while being our loving self entirely.

Rick Rescorla will never be forgotten, as he lives on in the hearts of those who have learned to follow him. God bless, one Rick Rescorla and those he so lovingly inspires.

FIRST LIEUTENANT NICHOLAS SNIDER (RET.)

Nick Snider, my dear friend has always been very supportive and done so much to honor Rick. Nick founded The National Museum of Patriotism in Atlanta, which featured Georgia's only exhibit of the September 11th terrorist attacks. The museum was recently transformed into the National Foundation of Patriotism, a virtual online museum, to "afford the mission a broader reach, deeper impact and higher visibility than could ever be attained by one building in one city." A retired vice president of United Parcel Service, Nick was an OCS classmate of Rick's at Fort Benning.

It was one of those rare opportunities in life in which your past brushes against your future in one tragic and surreal event that suspended the world in shock and disbelief. September 11, 2001, the most horrifying day in our recent history, America under attack on our own soil. We all have our memories of where we were and what we were doing that morning when we first learned of what was happening. I was watching television and was shocked when a plane flew into the South Tower, and shocked again to learn that Rick was inside the building.

As the dust and debris settled over the Manhattan horizon, many stories and accounts of heroism and sacrifice would abound. When the details of Rick's self-less and deliberate actions emerged, people learned of his extraordinary personal sacrifice, which resulted in saving thousands of lives. I know his act of unbridled heroism has and will continue to impact the hearts and minds of America's future heroes, and his story is one that will forever reside in the spirit of the greatest nation in the world.

Susan continues to carry the torch of love and fans the flame of his memory as she marches across America with her personal accounts of his life and heroism. Rick's story is a story America needs to remember. And Susan's efforts to keep Rick's memory alive for the benefit of strengthening the resolve of a grateful nation, are nothing less than heroic in their own right.

CAPTAIN MATTHEW DEMNY

A few years ago, I became aware that the Forward Operating Base in Farah, Afghanistan, had been named FOB Rescorla, in honor of Rick. Two soldiers stationed there painted a large mural showing different aspects of his life on the outside wall of one building. I was sent a DVD compiled by people at FOB Rescorla so I could see how they have been training Afghans to fight the Taliban, along with the great camaraderie among the soldiers themselves. I have tried helping them out in any way I can, sending candy, heavy-duty socks, goggles and copies of Heart of a Soldier.

I have received several emails from soldiers stationed there, expressing how honored they were to be stationed there. The sentiments range from " I am proud to say I'm living at FOB Rescorla, thank you so much for sharing your husband with us," to " I just hope and pray I am half the man he was," or "We owe him so much and I want you to know he is not forgotten."

At one point I received an email from Captain Matthew J. Demny, FOB Rescorla's Foreign Military Combat Advisor. Although I have never met Matt, we continue to correspond and will always be friends.

Team Yukon and I deployed in support of the Global War on Terrorism, for one hellish tour of duty. We were stationed at an outpost, in western Afghanistan in the Farah Province, called FOB Rescorla. We were charged with the responsibility of training, mentoring and coaching the Afghanistan National Army (ANA). Our challenges and struggles were many, but the rewards of seeing the ANA transition into a lethal, independent fighting force at the end of the deployment was well worth the countless hours of training provided to the soldiers of the ANA.

My Team and I received an orientation around the small FOB one day, and something that really caught my attention was a mural and patriotic message of a Warrior located on a wall of one of our buildings. As the days quickly passed, I became more and more intrigued with the story behind our FOB representation and the person in the mural. I researched Colonel (Ret.) Rick Rescorla and discovered an amazing story of one of America's warriors. I learned of the tremendous sacrifices he made in honor of our great Country. He sacrificed for our Country with sweat and blood and did not falter until the job was done . . . successfully.

In the latter portion of my deployment, I connected with Susan Rescorla and expressed how proud we were to be serving on the battlefield for our Country, and to be residing on a FOB humbly named after her courageous husband. Susan and I continued to correspond throughout my remaining days in Afghanistan, and have kept in touch to this day. I have never felt more joy and pride in my short-lived ten-year military career then I did when I resided on FOB Rescorla. Team Yukon's experience with the deployment, and during our conversations with Susan, have been truly humbling. Susan's unyielding efforts in displaying her husband's contributions to the United States of America are heart-felt and genuine. Rick's dedication, loyalty and devotion to the USA will never be forgotten.

LIEUTENANT BUD ALLEY (RET.)

Bud Alley served in Vietnam with Rick, and the two maintained a close relationship. Bud and his wife visited us at our home in New Jersey as well. Bud shared several heartfelt recollections of Rick, who he reconnected with some 25 years after serving together.

July 1965, I was the newly assigned Communications Officer for the 2nd Battalion 7th Cavalry. I was ordered to process security clearance requests for all of our new officers, including a group of Second

Lieutenants straight out of OCS. I didn't think it would be much of an issue, and I forwarded the requests up through channels. All were approved for secret classifications except for one guy who was singled out and not allowed to use any battalion radios or telephones. The guy was Cyril R. Rescorla. I called this Cyril R. Rescorla into my office where I somewhat routinely informed him that he was restricted from using any means of communication until I could investigate the matter further.

"Bloody Hell!" he retorted, his face reddening.

Now, as a southern born and bred fella, "bloody hell" was not a term I had ever heard before. But Cyril R. Rescorla was pretty big, seemed pretty pissed, talked funny, and certainly commanded my attention.

"Okay," I told him. "There must be some mistake and I'll get it resolved."

I then asked him where he was from.

"Cornwall," he replied.

"Never heard of it," I said.

"England, bloody England," he said.

"Well that must be the problem then, you are a foreigner!" I said. "But look, I will see what I can do to get things straightened out. In the meantime, try to keep a low profile."

So that was my initial encounter with one of the greatest soldier scholars there ever was. A few weeks later on board the USS Rose, Rick came up to me and inquired about his security clearance. I just smiled at him and he grinned back, replying, "What are they going to do to me? Send me to Vietnam?"

Over the course of the voyage, I heard a number of stories about Rick. It seems he was already a legend, having been a professional soldier before coming to the U.S. I understood his petulance about the clearance, and it was quietly dropped. I never did get an official notice of his security clearance that year.

The first time I flew in to deliver a message to his Commanding Officer, he had just come out of our first firefight, gotten his first Purple Heart, and made his first enemy kill. I approached the aid station where he was getting a bandage, and he said, smiling, "Look Alley, I got the bloody bastard alright. See, that's his brains right there on my helmet." And that was the beginning of the Rescorla marvel.

As the year went on, I never saw him without a smile, even under the grimmest circumstances. He was a leader, a warrior, all the stories that grew around him that year were true. The first organizer of a long-range patrol group, he handpicked his men, and they dropped into the combat area days ahead of our deployment to gather intelligence. Talk about balls! Jungle terrain, no radio communication for days, scouting around for enemy with only four men . . . day-umn. In the south, damn is always a two-syllable word.

The Officer's Club we built became a place where Rick would continue to amaze his fellow officers with his intellect, athleticism, and love for singing. Upon returning to our base and getting squared away, our only refuge was the "O Club." To break the monotony and boredom, we would often entertain ourselves with song. Rick sang with the gusto and gift of an opera singer. Oh, he was more than a hoot. He was outrageous with his knowing winks and broad smile.

And then, one rainy day, it was over. One minute he was there, and the next he was on the chopper headed out, and I lost track of him. Then, in the early 1990s, when Joe Galloway and Colonel Hal Moore were researching *We Were Soldiers Once . . . and Young*, I was contacted by Galloway and asked for Rick's phone number. I called, and suddenly an acquaintance that had lain dormant over 25 years was renewed. I wasn't sure he would remember me, but one of the first things he asked was if I had ever gotten his security clearance squared away, which got a big laugh from me.

Over those next few years we saw each other at reunions and swapped stories. Rick was still someone who made everyone feel like his best friend, and he went out of his way to be kind to me. At our 1992 reunion when the book was unveiled, I dragged my son with me to meet the men I served with. My son was at a stage in life where his father could not say any correct words, plus, he was failing out of college. But I got him to go to the reunion. I asked several of the guys to take a minute and speak with my son, in spite of his long hair. Rick, and Larry Gwin, and Skip Fesmire were most gracious and spent time with him. Now these men are legends, and for them to do this for me meant the world. All of them assured me that Mike would be OK.

Still, shortly after we returned, Mike dropped out of college and left to find himself in the ski country of Colorado. His mother and I tearfully watched him pack and leave. We weren't sure we would ever see him again. A week later, he called from Colorado. For some reason he had taken *We Were Soldiers Once . . . and Young*, with him, and he was reading it.

"Dad!" he exclaimed. "These guys all signed the book. I met them. I talked with them. Wow, I can't believe it! You were all heroes, especially Rick."

I smiled to myself, noting that he was now on a first name basis with one of the greatest men he would ever meet. I called Rick after hanging up with my son and thanked him for his kindness.

Over the next few years as our friendship renewed and grew, we learned that we were both knife collectors. I sent Rick a handmade knife from a South Carolina maker and got back a nice note. The next year at the reunion, Rick called me off to the side and placed a leather-covered item in my hand. He said look at it later. It was a knife with a bone handle, roughly scrimshawed with a map of all the Native American reservations. It is my most treasured possession and sits on top of my copy of *Heart of a Soldier*. But that was Rick. Quiet in his gift giving, always ready to help out. Always looking for something special in every person he met. He was always the one everyone of us trusted.

Rick knew I was a bit of a historian on the Civil War, and a picture taken of us at Gettysburg still sits on my shelf today. Every so often he would call to ask me a question about some arcane thing from American history. The discussion would end with Rick educating me how his question related to Napoleon, or Waterloo, or another battle I had limited knowledge of. He was always referencing poetry and we discussed his writing. He was without a doubt the most curious man I ever knew. He could speak on any topic you questioned him on. Not just on the surface, but meaningfully. Native Americans or Asian religions, it didn't matter, he could recite from their poetry or narratives. Renaissance man isn't a large enough way to describe this man.

For our first granddaughter's birthday on June 1, 2001, in Red Bank, New Jersey, we made plans to visit Rick and his new bride in Morristown. He made it easy to find his place by hanging his 7th Cavalry jacket out front. Ebullient, Rick bounded out to meet us. I don't think I have ever seen him so happily animated. He introduced his bride, Susan, to us and bowed slightly as he did so. Their love for one another was really wonderful to see. I know Rick had experienced his share of life's bumps, and the change in him since our last meeting was miraculous. They both glowed when they looked at one another. If I hadn't known better, I would have said they were like teenagers in puppy love, it was so obvious.

We listened to the story of their courtship, which was so Rick Rescorla. Him running barefoot to see what it felt like to a person he was trying to write about. Susan, walking her beloved dog, startled to see a grown man running barefoot along the walkway. Soon they realized they had finally found the one person in the universe who understood them perfectly. It wasn't a long courtship. Rick wasn't going to let this opportunity get by, and neither was Susan. This man was like a dream from King Arthur's court. He danced, he sang, he wrote poetry. She didn't know his warrior past at first. Our visit was one of the first she had seen of his past come into their home. She was pleased. We made plans to rendezvous in late fall in the Delaware Valley to roam the art and B&B community

After a sumptuous meal and conversation about art, and history, and children, we had to leave. Before he would let me go though, he said he had something for me. He knew I had spent a career in the corrugated box business. He placed a cloth bag in my hands. Inside the bag was a beautiful wooden box. The kind you keep on your dresser, the kind you keep your watches in, your precious jewels, and your memories.

The evening of 9/11, about six o'clock, I made that dreaded call to Susan. I was hoping against hope that he had taken the day off, that they had gone for a drive in the country, but somehow, deep down inside, I was afraid that I had lost a friend. His box is still on my dresser and not a day goes by that I don't thank God for the privilege of counting Rick Rescorla as a friend.

Later that fall, I drove with Susan to the Raptor Center where we sat in silence on a bench in front of two glorious American Bald Eagles that had been rescued from injury. Sitting there in silence, I couldn't help but see how majestically they represented my friend Rick. They had been through trauma, they had been hurt, but through it all, they remained erect, poised, defiant and proud. So Rick. Unbowed, unbroken, that look in their gaze that said, "We will never surrender."

CHAPTER 5

Sharing Rick With the World

*R*ick's story has been inspirational to a number of filmmakers, writers, artists and musicians. Their work is dear to my heart because it is through them that Rick's legacy lives on.

Rick's role in 9/11 became significantly more visible with the airing of "Unsung Hero," on Dateline NBC, with Jane Pauley, broadcast in March 2002. Described by NBC as an episode that "chronicles the life of Vietnam War and 9/11 hero Rick Rescorla," the program dedicated three segments to depict Rick's early life, including his upbringing in Hayle, England, his years as a soldier, focusing on the Battle of Ia Drang Valley, and his heroism on 9/11. Rick was a humble man and I was thankful that Jane Pauley noted early in the program that Rick "wasn't a man who lived for glorification."

The broadcast featured interviews with Mervyn Sullivan, Dan Hill, men who fought with Rick in Vietnam including his radioman Sam Fantino, a Morgan Stanley employee and myself. I think the depth of our relationship came across when I was asked to express my feelings about Rick.

"He was the love of my life," I said, crying.

"We did not spend a day apart. He emailed me poems, brought home flowers, my life was filled with passion and romance."

Mervyn explained how Rick's tendency to sing, even under dire circumstances, was simply a customary response inherent in the Cornish upbringing. One soldier who served with him in Vietnam said Rick's singing during a battle had a steadying influence on the men in their foxholes.

"I thought if he can do that, the least I can do is be manly, be a better soldier," he said.

Sam said Rick was often called "Hard Core" in Vietnam not as a nickname, but because "that's who he was." Sam also said that as his radioman, he was literally connected to Rick by a wire, adding: "It was more like an umbilical cord because wherever he went, I had to go, which was always up front. Rick never followed, he led his men."

The Morgan Stanley employee described how Rick began evacuation drills soon after being hired, but some people were reluctant to participate, and many considered them a waste of time. The employee pointed out how the attitude changed significantly following the 1993 garage bomb.

When the History Channel first broadcast in September 2005 The Man Who Predicted 9/11, *the documentary provided a comprehensive overview of Rick's terrorist concerns, and examined the steps he took to get people out of the South Tower. Several Morgan Stanley employees, Dan Hill, Fred McBee and myself, were among those interviewed. The documentary continues to air periodically, usually around 9/11 each year. I have a sense when it has been broadcast because it often triggers emails to the Rick Rescorla Memorial Website from viewers expressing their support and appreciation of Rick's heroism.*

I have always tried to be responsive when others were moved to learn more about Rick. I appreciate the time that the following people took to share with me how Rick was and continues to be a source of inspiration.

JAMES B. STEWART

In December 2001, I received a message on my answering machine from Jim Stewart explaining that he wanted to write a story about Rick for The New Yorker *magazine. At the time, I did not know that Jim, an author and business columnist for the* New York Times, *was a former editor for the* Wall Street Journal, *not to mention having won a Pulitzer Prize for his nonfiction book,* Den of Thieves, *about insider trading on Wall Street. I agreed to meet with him and we made arrangements for him to interview me at my home in Morristown.*

I picked Jim up at the train station, drove to my townhouse and we went inside to talk. Jim ended up writing an incredible article, The Real Heroes Are Dead, A Love Story, *that appeared in the February 2002 issue of* The New Yorker. *Jim visited several times and I kept saying there needed to be a book about Rick and asked if he would write it, and I would write the epilogue. After several discussions, Jim agreed and Simon & Schuster published* Heart of a Soldier, A Story of Love, Heroism, and September 11th, *in November 2002.*

When a copy of Heart of a Soldier *arrived at my home, I could not open up the book. I carried it into my car and drove around. Over the years I read pieces of it, eventually reading the entire book. I thank Jim so much for writing* Heart of a Soldier *and his support over the years.*

81

Rick's life and death, and his deep love for Susan, touched on the deepest themes of human existence, distilled through the prism of the greatest tragedy of my lifetime. In fact, the day after the World Trade Center collapsed, I was sitting in my apartment when I received a call from the editor of *The New Yorker*, David Remnick, saying something like, "You're our Wall Street person, go down there." So I did. As I went about my work as a reporter on Wall Street with the smoldering ruins of the World Trade Center in the background, I heard about the remarkable escape of approximately 3,000 Morgan Stanley employees. Somebody mentioned to me that it was sort of mysterious that almost nobody had been killed from Morgan Stanley, the World Trade Center's largest tenant, even though many people on the floors above and below were wiped out.

Three or four weeks later, I was at a dinner and happened to bring this up, and somebody sitting next to me connected to Wall Street said, "Oh, you know, there was some guy who was head of security at Morgan Stanley who got them all out." I decided to call Morgan Stanley, and a spokeswoman told me that the firm would have no comment and wasn't interested in having any stories written about its role at the World Trade Center. I was about to hang up thinking this was a dead end, when the person added: "If I were you, I would call Susan Rescorla, and here's her unlisted number in New Jersey."

It was a difficult call to make, but I did, and Susan agreed to see me. When she picked me up at the train station she was very gracious and seemed fairly calm, given the circumstances. We went to the townhouse that her and Rick had shared in Morristown and I was greeted by her beloved Golden Retriever Buddy. Rick's shoes were still by the door, and I remember when a phone call came in at one point, his voice was still on their answering machine.

Susan showed me some pictures and talked about Rick and it wasn't long before she was crying, and within moments, I was crying too. It was a very emotional experience. As Rick's story unfolded, Susan and I worked through most of a box of tissues. Two hours later when I was on the train back to New York I looked at my notebook and realized I hadn't written a word.

That was the beginning of what turned into *The New Yorker* article, *The Real Heroes Are Dead, A Love Story*, that focused on the unbelievably close relationship between Rick and Susan, a relatively late in life romance over the course of the last three years or so of his life. As it turned out, Rick was working on an autobiography, and in reviewing some of his material, it was amazing to read his profound thoughts about the nature of heroism, courage and the obligations we have to our fellow man. The tentative title for his autobiography was *Heart of a Soldier*, which was the obvious title to use for the book I was eventually to write.

There was tremendous heroism by many that day, but Rick's was virtually unique from what I knew. This was a mystery, difficult to understand. I wanted to know what kind of person he was and why would he make the choice to risk his own life and face almost certain death to save others. I also recognized this in its broad outlines as one of the most elemental stories told throughout human history, and that's the story of a human being who chooses to give up their own life for others, suggesting there are causes in life more important than our own individual survival. That has been at the heart of many stories told throughout mankind.

Rick was a soldier trained to follow orders, yet he defied Port Authority orders that people stay at their desks and got his people out.

By remaining in the World Trade Center, Rick chose duty over self-interest. He made a heroic decision. He was under no obligation to go back up into that inferno and yet he did. He could have left the World Trade Center then and there and been acclaimed a hero, and he would be alive today. Yet, for some reason, he went back and gave his life trying to save others.

In reading through his writings, it was clear that Rick was a man still striving to become more, questioning if he had achieved all he could have achieved. I try and think about that every day. Have I done all I can do every day with the qualities that have been bestowed on me? That to me in the end is the message I took from Rick, and in the end is the message I hope will inspire others.

ROBERT EDWARDS

The writer/director Robert Edwards first feature film, Land of the Blind, *starred Ralph Fiennes and Donald Sutherland, and won the Nicholl Fellowship in Screenwriting from the Academy of Motion Picture Arts and Sciences in 2001. Robert was a budding filmmaker in 1998 when he interviewed Rick for a documentary he was working on about the Battle of Ia Drang Valley. Robert's father was in the military and fought with Rick in the Battle of Ia Drang.*

Raised on Army bases across the country, Robert became an army intelligence officer and captain in a parachute infantry regiment in the first Gulf War before eventually deciding to become a filmmaker. After graduating from Stanford University's Master's Program in Documentary Film, Robert decided to make a documentary about the

Battle of Ia Drang Valley, and contacted Rick who agreed to an interview at his office.

During the interview, Rick happened to express his concerns about future terrorist attacks. Shortly after 9/11, Robert reviewed the footage of his interview with Rick, and from that he edited an eight-minute segment which he called The Voice of the Prophet. *The piece consisted of Rick talking straight into the camera about the probability of the events that did indeed end up leading to September 11th. "The Voice of the Prophet" was subsequently viewed at the Sundance, Toronto, and Human Rights Watch Film Festivals, and has been excerpted on television around the world.*

I have become friends with Robert and his wife Ferne Perlstein (also an outstanding filmmaker), and am glad to have them in my life.

Rick and my father fought together in the Battle of Ia Drang Valley. In the early 1990s, around the time the book *We Were Soldiers Once . . . and Young* came out, I attended a reunion of 7th Calvary veterans with my dad and heard Rick speak to the group. He was incredibly charismatic and compelling.

A few years later, I had become a documentary filmmaker and was trying to make a documentary about the battle. I knew from the start that Rick would be one of the key interview subjects, as one of the only officers to have been at both LZ X-xay and LZ Albany, not to mention his fascinating personal history, and having seen for myself what a great speaker he was.

In July 1998, I flew from San Francisco, where I was based at the time, to New York to interview him. To shoot that interview I hired a New York-based documentary cinematographer named Ferne

Pearlstein. The interview was to be conducted in Rick's Morgan Stanley office in the South Tower of the World Trade Center. As we drove into the underground parking garage in a rented van loaded with cases full of camera equipment, Ferne and I recalled the 1993 World Trade Center bombing, and noted that the building's security — while superficially thorough — was not really airtight. If we had been terrorists bent on doing damage, we might easily have slipped through.

We met Rick and set up our lights and equipment in his South Tower office, the Manhattan skyline and the Empire State Building visible through the big window behind where Rick was seated. In the interview he talked eloquently about his experiences in Cyprus, Rhodesia, and Vietnam, about the Ia Drang Battle, and about what he saw as the future of warfare. His comments were just as powerful as I had expected, and he gave several profound quotes that I instantly knew were destined to be in the finished film.

At one point during the interview, while we were changing camera magazines, Rick asked if Ferne and I were a couple. Ferne replied that we were not; that we had just met. The tape recorder was running and those comments were captured on tape. But Rick, very perceptively, must have intuited something in our dynamic. Ferne and I were both exhausted, having only slept a few hours after staying up talking the whole night before — our first "date," so to speak. To make a long story short, Ferne and I began dating that very week, and I soon moved from California to New York to be with her. Three years later we were married.

It was only two and a half weeks before our wedding day that the hijacked airplanes crashed into the Twin Towers. Then, as now, Ferne and I lived in Lower Manhattan; I heard the first explosion and saw the second one. We watched the towers burning from the roof of our apartment building, only about a mile and a half from what would soon be known as Ground Zero. As we tried to account for the safety of the various people we knew who might have been at the site of the attack, we of course thought of Rick. On our wall we still had a framed black-and-white photograph of the Twin Towers that Rick had given Ferne three years before at the completion of his interview, and which he autographed for her as a memento of the occasion.

Within a few days we learned that he had been killed, and about his heroic actions on that terrible day. That he had saved the lives of so many of his co-workers — both through his actions that morning and through his foresight in planning for such a contingency — came as no surprise to us, knowing the kind of man he was.

My documentary about the Battle of Ia Drang Valley was never finished: in part because an ABC news program beat me to the punch, and in part because I became distracted by my new cross-country love affair. I put all the footage in storage and largely forgot about it. But after we learned of Rick's death I got his interview out again and watched it for the first time since 1998. I was stunned, having forgotten precisely what he had said on camera, and realizing now how prescient he had been: predicting that the future of war would be terrorism, that there would be attacks on American soil that would circumvent the United States' great military power, and that the mistakes of U.S. foreign policy would come home to roost. He was absolutely prophetic.

I realized that people had to hear Rick's words. I quickly cut together an edited version of his interview — simply him speaking directly into the camera for eight minutes, nothing more. It was my great honor to show that short film in public for the first time at the annual reunion of

Ia Drang veterans in November 2001, only two months after the 9/11 attacks, and to meet Rick's widow Susan at that event. For many people in the room, hearing Rick's voice and seeing his image on film was like being visited by a ghost. With Susan's blessing, that short documentary went on to be seen by millions of people at the Sundance Film Festival and numerous other festivals, on nationwide U.S. and international television, and to this day, on the Internet. It was my great privilege to help the profound words of this true American hero be heard.

It was a great honor to have known Rick, if only briefly, and to have him touch our lives. He was not only a hero but also a true Renaissance man of tremendous passion and wisdom, whose larger-than-life personality left an impression on everyone with whom he ever crossed paths. In addition to the photograph he signed for us, Ferne and I still have the audio cassette with Rick's voice asking, "Is this a husband and wife team?" and Ferne replying, "No, we just met." Now that we have been married for almost 10 years, and have a daughter together, that recording is more meaningful to us than ever.

ROGER GRAEF

The National Center for Victims of Crime invited me to speak when it decided to honor Rick at its 2002 Annual Leadership Award ceremony at Bryant Park in Manhattan, and that's where I first met Roger Graef. A native New Yorker, Roger moved to London in 1962, and has become a highly regarded filmmaker. Roger was awarded a BAFTA (British Academy of Film and Television Arts) Fellowship, the highest honor the Academy presents, putting him in the company of luminaries like Alfred Hitchcock, Louis Malle, Stanley Kubrick and Steven Spielberg. His work ranges from documentaries, including Police, *which is credited with changing the way police in the UK investigate rape cases, and* Requiem for Detroit? *to Amnesty International's* Secret Policeman's Ball *and the first* Comic Relief *charity fundraising event.*

Roger's Films of Record production company was making a documentary that focused on families who lost loved ones in 9/11 called September Mourning, *and I ended up being one of the people interviewed. People from Roger's company met me at London's Paddington railway station, and we took the train to Cornwall for some of the filming. Additional filming was done in this country, including my home. Over the years, Roger has become a great, supportive friend. Roger and his daughter Chloe have visited me at my home and, if even only through email or phone, we have remained in touch all these years.*

When I met Susan, who was speaking at an event honoring Rick, the people I was sitting with had such a solidarity, so obviously admired and loved Rick, it was a special privilege to be around them, and then to be around Susan as well. I try and keep in touch with many of the people in my documentaries, but the depth of the relationship that I have developed with Susan is unusual. We are friends and we will be friends forever. I admire her so much.

Obviously, the tragedy of 9/11 itself was stunning, and as an American living in Britain I felt strongly about it. But while the focus was almost entirely on New York, the people in New York, and all the American's lost, I also felt it was an international event, and my first thought was that I would look at how many other countries had people killed on

9/11 and their reaction. But then I thought, the thing untouched by anybody would be the mourning period, the grief, over the next year. So instead of the international approach, I decided to follow four families who had lost somebody in the tragedy and that is what I did over the next year. The title is just a play on words, as a normal September morning became a September Mourning, but it felt like a poetic title to me and I liked it.

When I was in New York looking for people for the documentary, I happened to stop somewhere to have my hair cut. I asked if anyone in the shop knew of someone who had been directly impacted by the tragedy. The woman cutting my hair said her best friend had lost her father. The father was a security guard, and he is the black man whose back you see in the picture of Rick talking into the megaphone during the evacuation. It was pure chance, an amazing coincidence, that both families were represented in the film.

The heroism of Rick on that day was astounding. Sacrificing himself to save others was incredibly brave. What was most poignant was that he warned his company after the first bombing in 1993 that the building was not secure and that if the terrorists had been more adroit, they would have done more damage. The fact that he knew that, anticipated it, yet wasn't able to persuade the authorities to do anything about it, and then the moment came and he scarified himself for others, is a kind of exemplary heroism that one very rarely comes across.

The station that broadcast *September Mourning*, ITV, is a commercial network. Yet, to ITV's huge credit, they gave up all advertising to show the piece at its true length, 63 minutes, rather than interrupting it with commercials and cutting it down to 48 minutes. It was a big debate at the time, but they understood the significance of what we were doing, and afterwards, their director of programming said he was prouder of airing that documentary than any he had ever previously shown.

MARK FORD

Mark Ford was formerly a reporter for the Western Daily Press, *a regional newspaper in Bristol, whose coverage area includes Cornwall. Mark did an outstanding job writing articles about Rick and even came to my home in Morristown for an interview. Mark also presented me with a commemorative gold coin which had both the American and Cornish flags on one side, and the words " A Tribute From Western Daily Press Readers to Rick Rescorla. March 15, 2006." Mark and I continue corresponding and I am sure we will always remain friends.*

Rick Rescorla's circumstances were obviously extraordinary, but I initially worked on this story with some reluctance. I had always hated the 'death knock' aspect of journalism — the grim term for imposing yourself on people who had lost loved ones and turning grief or outrage into a story — but that was before I had the chance to speak with and eventually meet Susan. Susan's commitment to Rick and his memory are as infectious as Rick's story is remarkable. As a result, continuing the recognition of Rick through several articles, and introducing his story to new people has always felt positive and constructive.

I corresponded by email and phone with Susan, and eventually met her at her home in Morristown — an unexpected editor's instruction with only a couple of days notice. Susan made me, and my photographer, feel more welcome than we had any right to expect. Along with the usual family photographs that she showed us, Rick's name was still on the answering machine, and a pair of his shoes still by the front door. I did the interview and we took the necessary photographs.

By the time we left, I no longer felt that I had imposed myself on someone beaten by grief or driven by anger. I felt that I had been fortunate enough to spend time with someone with a humbling devotion to a lost loved one, and a determination to tell as many people as possible about him to make sure his heroic actions are not forgotten.

My involvement was miniscule and short-lived, but after all of this, I am aware of having had a tiny role in Rick and Susan's "story," a story which is itself bound up in events that changed the world.

PETE ALTIERI

Pete Altieri is the founder of the Bloomington, Illinois based heavy metal band Low 12. Pete is the band's bass player and singer. He first learned of Rick while touring. He was in his hotel room and happened to see The Man Who Predicted 9/11 *on the History Channel. Pete was a 7th Cavalry veteran himself, having served in the Gulf War, and was moved to write* A Hero's Last Stand *in Rick's honor, and the band has also performed a live "Tribute to Rick Rescorla" concert.*

On 9/11/08 I was sitting in a hotel room and saw *The Man Who Predicted 9/11* on the History Channel. I was completely blown away by Rick's story and felt compelled to write a song about it. We were in the writing process for our *Splatter Pattern* CD and I felt strongly about doing something in tribute to Rick's incredible life story. Oddly enough — I was also in the 7th Cavalry, but during the Desert Storm era.

So when this idea came to me — it almost seemed like I was meant to write the song about Rick and spread the message. I did quite a bit of research including talking with Susan and Fred McBee. Fred sent us some rare Vietnam audio to use on the song, which features Rick and fellow 7th Cavalry officers singing while off duty in 1966, only months after the infamous Battle of Ia Drang Valley. When our song *A Hero's Last Stand* was born, it ended up being one of the strongest on our CD. Rick is a true American hero.

A HERO'S LAST STAND

A hero's last stand
The world starts to crumble, he's got the plan
He faced evil when others ran
A hero's last stand

Enamored as a boy, with soldiers on parade
To march with pride, as medals shine, and people call your name
The Ia Drang in '65, his valor saved countless lives
The ones who fell would haunt his dreams until his final breath

Infectious personality, he left his mark on all he knew
His job now meant he was security in Tower Two
He trained them well as they faced Hell, his voice cutting the din
Predictions came true, Rescorla knew how things would end that day

Others freeze and panic
Courage cuts the chaos
Hero rises from the ashes, hero rises from the ashes!

He could have gotten out alive
But he stayed to help his fellow man
2,694 were saved by the hero on the stairs
He made his last stand

ROY RAY

In 2009 I was contacted by the St. Ives based artist Roy Ray. Roy had created a series of mixed media panels titled Evilution: Where Their Footsteps Left No Trace. *One of the panels involved his reaction to 9/11. Roy was coming to New York to do more work and was hoping that we could meet at some point. I was not familiar with Roy's work, but I certainly was aware that St. Ives, a seaside town in Cornwall that Rick and I loved and visited often. I told Roy I would be delighted to meet with him.*

Roy arrived in 2010, and we spent a wonderful day together, and the next time I visited Cornwall we met again. I stayed at Roy and his wife Beryl's home for five days, and we have all become good friends. Roy and I drove to view the installation of the panels for an exhibition at the Coventry Cathedral. We also visited the Barbara Hepworth Museum and Sculpture Garden, which I loved so much during my visits with Rick.

Roy's panels are a powerful statement about man's inhumanity to man and were featured at a Ground Zero exhibition at St. Peter's

Church in New York, in July 2011. With its close proximity to the World Trade Center, St. Peter's Church was a staging area during the 9/11 rescue and recovery operations, and where the body of Father Mychal Judge, the Chaplin for the New York City Fire Department and 9/11's "Victim 0001," was laid before the altar by his fellow firefighters. At the Ground Zero exhibition the panels were blessed by Father Kevin Madigan and dedicated to Father Judge, the first responders, and Rick.

I have many childhood memories of growing up near London at the time of the Blitz, the earliest being of my father digging a huge hole in our garden. Many years later, in a conversation with him just before he died, he told me that the hole was meant to serve as an air raid shelter for our family, as he was about to be called for military service. Nightly bombing raids became regular and although only four years old, I sensed that something bad was happening and began to know fear. I was also growing up with an acceptance that the sounds of war were the norm — a way of life.

Following the death of my father, more of those early memories began surfacing and a friend encouraged me to write them down, remarking that I was writing poetry and should continue. From those early memories and the many newsreels of the war that I have since viewed, I coined the word *Evilution* to describe our ability to make great advances in science and technology only to turn them into the means of killing.

Then 9/11 happened, and I couldn't believe that what I had been writing about, events that happened so many years ago, were happening again, now, that I was watching an evil, tragic situation unfolding right before me eyes on television. And then the Cornwall newspapers told us about Rick Rescorla being a local man and the role he played in 9/11, and there was a kind of collective, "Oh my God, we've lost Rick," that I think we all felt. The events of 9/11 catapulted me into action and although I had spent most of my working life painting the landscape of West Cornwall, I felt I now had to make something tangible as a direct response to 9/11 — this latest example of *Evilution*.

The towers were so symbolic of these advances in technology so I knew that was the theme, but also, for me, cell phones became a major focus. The cell phones were central to the piece because for so many people, the last conversation that people had with their loved ones was on a cell phone. That was the bit that really got to me the most. I found that very moving. I went to a local cell phone company and persuaded them to give me lots of cell phones. I began pulling together pieces of wiring, cables and the cell phones, and arranging them onto a panel. I surprised myself when I finished as I realized that 9/11 had unleashed something deep inside of me.

It took me until about 2006 to complete the five panels, which is my personal response to events in my lifetime in which our capacity to harness invention and technology has been used to destroy life on a massive scale. But I'm coming to it as a child who grew up in wartime, not a clever historian, which I'm not. The underlying essence of the panels is not about conflict or who is to blame, it's about the innocent victims who were in the wrong place at the wrong time through no fault of their own, and all of them meant something to someone else, and now there is no trace of them.

The project has become more personal because it has put me into direct contact with so many people who have suffered, and at the top of that list is Susan. I have been very taken with her determination to have Rick fully recognized for all he did, and also very much taken with her warmth. What has touched me as I've gotten to know her is the sheer depth of her loss, and the deep level of her and Rick's relationship. They were so incredibly close; they enjoyed living with each other, just being in each other's company, and then it was taken away.

I am planning to make more works about Rick. Rick was a warrior, a man who was such a leader, who in a war could never leave a man behind, and reverted to that same leader on 9/11. He was a well-read man who loved Shakespeare, Kipling and was in the midst of an extraordinarily powerful love story with Susan. I am not a religious person, I don't attend church, but for some reason this man from Cornwall and I have crossed paths. Rick and I have the same initials, we were both born on May 27th, and out of nowhere, Rick and Susan have come into my life. I do not understand it, all I can do is accept it. But my hope is that this is another step in my aim, as an artist, to get people to think more about the destruction of innocent lives. I want people to stop and think, to remember those whose lives were lost, the heroes like Rick Rescorla, but also the anonymous victims, the forgotten souls – those whose footsteps left no trace.

COLONEL WILLIAM "WILL" MERRILL (RET.)

The Chase-Rescorla Scholarship Fund was created in 2007 to raise money to help low-income students further their education. It is named in honor of Rick and Leo C. Chase Jr., who both fought in the Battle of Ia Drang Valley. Sadly, Mr. Chase was killed in action. I was attending the annual dinner when I first met William "Will" Merrill, a West Point alumni, and his wife Barbara. Since our initial meeting we have become great friends. I have visited them in their beautiful brownstone home in Brooklyn, New York, in Florida, and in 2010 was a guest at their timeshare in Marbella, Spain.

Along with being a West Point graduate, Will is a retired Colonel, having served 31 distinguished years in the military. Will has written a book about 9/11 entitled Ordinary People: Extraordinary Heroes *that was recently published and focuses on the role first responders played that day, and why our country must not become complacent with respect to the war on terror. His book includes an introduction by New York Senator Peter King, an interview with former Mayor Rudy Giuliani, and an entire chapter devoted to Rick's life story.*

Although I never had the privilege of meeting Rick Rescorla, he was clearly a very brave and very astute man. Everyone that I interviewed about 9/11 knew of Rick Rescorla and certainly his life story further inspired me in writing *Ordinary People: Extraordinary Heroes.*

Rick clearly understood that the most challenging part of dealing with the war on terror is that the enemy is not some country, but rather consists of tiny cells that can be located anywhere. It certainly scares the hell out of me. Our enemy can now be just a small number of people who can inflict considerable damage. It only took 19 people on 9/11 to kill 3,000 others.

The South Tower was not very conducive to mass evacuation. The stairwells were only 44 inches wide. That is not a lot of room when you have firefighters and police rushing up the stairs while thousands of workers are going down the stairs during the course of an emergency.

Yet, because of Rick's insistence that everyone practice and participate in evacuation drills, his people did not panic and exited the building in an orderly manner. That kind of behavior is highly unusual. In fact, when I interviewed Mayor Giuliani, he said that often when there are bomb scares, people in the building are not told. Most bomb scares are false alarms, and law enforcement is worried people will panic and inadvertently get injured or killed while rushing to evacuate. To me, that illustrates how significant Rick's role was on 9/11 in saving thousands of lives.

The fact that after his job was already done he went back to rescue strangers who may have still been inside was above and beyond the call of duty. I was personally touched by the bravery of this man who knew he was in grave danger, yet stood up to face that danger when he could have easily walked away from the situation knowing he was already a hero. Rick joined people he didn't even know or was responsible for and died fighting by their sides.

MELODY MOORE

Melody Moore is a soprano who sang my role as Rick's wife in the opera Heart of A Soldier *which premiered on the 10-year anniversary of 9/11, and was presented by the San Francisco Opera Company. Melody has a beautiful spirit, and we bonded almost immediately. I also liked that she's taller than me because I always wanted to be taller.*

Melody is a much sought after Mimi in La Boheme, *and has sung the role with the San Francisco Opera, the English National Opera in a production by Jonathan Miller and with Opera Cleveland. She has appeared with the Los Angeles Opera as the Countess Almaviva in* Le Nozze di Figaro, *performed as Donna Elvira in* Don Giovanni *at Lincoln Theatre in Napa Valley and sung the title role in* Suor Angelica *for the Opera Theatre and Musical Festival of Lucca, Italy.*

When I went to San Francisco in September 2010 to watch some early Heart of a Soldier *workshops, I think I spent every day crying when I heard Melody sing. Her voice is so beautiful and the arias she sings are real dialogue between Rick and myself. Melody's performance truly captures the essence of my feelings for Rick. The experience of being part of Rick's story has deepened Melody's appreciation of people serving in the military, and also inspired her to do more than ever to help our soldiers.*

There are many people I consider to be heroes. My mother is a hero to me because she was able to raise three children on a private school teacher's income. But I have never known a hero in the proportion of Rick Rescorla. From what I've read and what Susan has told me, he always seemed to be looking for a way to go further, to do more for people, even if it brought danger or death, which of course it did. But Rick was built like that from the beginning, even as a child, and I have been very touched by this.

The opera, like the book, is about love, hope, faith, timing and trust, and that's why it's a great story. Susan met Rick at exactly the right time, and met him in a way that is unexplainable, serendipitous, and at the moment that was exactly right for her soul. She has had to feel a depth of pain that few people experience, but I can tell you that from my view from the outside, she got to meet the love of her life at exactly the right time and she is grateful for that. I have not lost a partner, a soulmate, but I did loose my father very tragically, so we have some language of loss that's the same.

The music in the opera was difficult, yet not depleting. In fact, I felt energized because I heard Rick's words and felt his personality and his spirit, and it makes me want to be better at everything. It is like I am receiving some kind of gift from him.

It has been an honor to be involved in this project. The experience has raised my awareness for those soldiers serving three, four, five tours of duty in Iraq or Afghanistan. I now think about these men and women and realize that there are many more things we can do to reach out to them and their families. I have made a commitment to become involved in a way that I was not before, even if that just means visiting soldiers returning from the service who live in my community so they do not feel forgotten or cut off. The opera came at the right time and right place for me. I felt like Rick was there and even though he lost his life, his spirit cannot be destroyed. This experience has changed me in a way that I am no longer willing to be a bystander.

THOMAS HAMPSON

Thomas Hampson, a baritone and protégé of the late Leonard Bernstein, sung the role of Rick in the San Francisco Opera Company premiere of Heart of a Soldier. *A favorite soloist of many conductors, Thomas has appeared throughout the world in virtually every major opera house and concert hall. Among his many roles are Mozart's* Don Giovanni, *Rossini's* Guillaume Tell, *Ambroise Thomas'* Hamlet *and Tchaikovsky's* Eugene Onegin. *In 2003, a recording of Wagner's*

Tannhauser with Thomas received a Grammy Award for Best Opera Recording.

I first met Thomas in February 2011 at a press conference in Manhattan for the opera. I immediately told him how his build was perfect for the role of Rick. As we talked, I was even more thrilled that he was singing the role since he definitely has the same type of charismatic personality that Rick had. It was easy speaking with him and he was clearly curious to learn more about Rick, and made a genuine connection with me, which included visiting me at my home with his lovely wife Andrea.

Most importantly, the opera and Rick's story was something that Thomas truly wanted to be involved with. Thomas was so respectful of Rick, his patriotism, his intelligence, his connection to others, I could not think of anybody better suited to sing the role of my husband.

Sometimes I have to pinch myself, this guy born in Indiana who grew up in Spokane, Washington, standing there singing the role of Shakespeare's *Hamlet* or having a dialogue with God in Ferruccio Busoni's *Dr. Faustus*. These and many other operas are epic stories, and the guys in them are pretty complex with some kind of major flaw. Finding out who these people are either slowly unravels or explodes in the context of learning the work I am singing. In any event, there is always a serious dose of humility involved in piecing their lives together, which is incredibly important.

The kind of completely unblemished hero found in Rick Rescorla is unusual in the opera world. Rick appeared to be a normal man, yet in many ways he did not fit into the contemporary world. We don't usually think of military people as having his degree of compassion and sensitivity. He breaks out of that mold. Rick was a man's man who liked to sit around the fire reading poetry and great literature.

I love the fact that he took creative writing courses and loved singing, and when a situation becomes difficult, whether during the horrifying battles in Vietnam or on 9/11, he quotes lines of poetry, or breaks out into a Cornwall song. I suppose a tune would come to his mind that centered him and in turn the people around him, so they could withstand the kind of horrors that would have made the rest of us crumble into bread cakes and be done with. I love the fact that he found a way to galvanize this zone of thought that enabled him to rise to such extraordinary heights. This warrior, husband, statesman, strong guy, literature loving man had the heart of a soldier, and that is a beautiful statement to him. It's the poetry, the words, the symbols, the sounds and the music that kept him going, centered his life, and I find that very touching.

Other than being somewhat similar to him physically, strong, with good posture, and polite, I couldn't be farther from Rick Rescorla if I tried. I did not serve in the military, did not have those kinds of experiences. On 9/11, like everyone else, I was just waking up and turned on CNN and thought I was watching a movie at first. I was in New York for rehearsals at the Metropolitan Opera, and the fire station by me on 66th and 10th was one of the first responders to the scene. They lost almost everyone, which was just horrible. That's about as close as I came. But even for Rick, it isn't necessarily the events and his role in them, but more his decency, his readiness to be reasonable and helpful to people around him that is so overwhelming to me. I find that decency, that core integrity is something I cling to. He was just this incredibly decent person who did the right thing.

The fact that he found true love late in life and that his life ends in a tragic and heroic way is also incredible. But being Rick Rescorla, I don't think there was ever a seed of doubt that he had to go back up into that tower. I can't imagine he would have done anything else. He is somebody I would have been very honored to meet and to know. Rick's foundation is the honest to God true values of human kindness and decency. This guy was built on stone and that's fantastic. The idea of the continuation of a spiritual existence, regardless of physical being — that realization that we as human beings somehow have to find in this life — even though we cannot possibly understand it, I find those kind of questions reinforcing and beautiful. In that sense, Rick's departure from this earth is as glorious as one could possibly hope to be allowed.

Rick's life has become a fundamental part of my life. I know of no other contemporary story of a great hero, a great human being that gives me more faith in humanity and can serve as an example to me. It is moving to be part of a process that will help so many others have some kind of relationship to Rick Rescorla. He was bigger than life in life, and he is now being immortalized after his life, and I think that's beautiful. Is there any more powerful way to explain the wonder and necessity of arts and humanities than this very process? It is the essence of what we do, retelling the stories of people's lives so we learn and can be encouraged, and even warned by them, and it is a living and real process. It is very exciting that Rick, in ways that he couldn't possibly have known, will have a continued influence on people. All of this is a deeply powerful and invigorating process. Rick's life story is sometimes overwhelming to me, and I'm not exaggerating when I say that I just hope I have done justice to him in *Heart of a Soldier*.

HANK FELLOWS

I first met Hank Fellows at Arlington County Fire Department's Fire Station 5, as part of another Iron and Steel ride. A native New Yorker, Hank is a songwriter who was living in New Jersey, across the Hudson River and witnessed the immediate aftermath of the destruction of the World Trade Center. Hank wrote The Spirit of America, *describing it as "a love song to my grief-stricken country." Then, struggling to come to terms with the murder of so many innocent people, he wrote* Halfway to Heaven. *These and many of Hank's other patriotic songs are often sung in schools, houses of worship and civic organizations.* Halfway to Heaven *was chosen by the New York City Fire Department as the soundtrack for its official video memorial honoring the 343 FDNY members murdered on 9/11. Hank's music was also performed at the July 2011 Ground Zero exhibition at St. Peter's Church.*

HALFWAY TO HEAVEN

On a bright September morning in the greatest city known,
A gentle breeze was blowing through the place they called their home,
And high above the city, they were working side by side,
In the gleaming towers reaching far up to the sky.

They were Halfway to Heaven and I know they're all there now,
Fathers, sons, and daughters, and mothers free and proud,
And those who raced into the flames to save their fellow man,
I know that they're all home now.

105

They will always be among us for their love can never die,
And we shall walk together though the years will all pass by,
And at ev'ry graduation, and wherever love is true,
Set a place at the table, for they will be there too.

They were Halfway to Heaven, and I know they're all there now,
Fathers, sons, and daughters, and mothers free and proud,
And those who raced into the flames to save their fellow man,
I know that they're all home now, I know that they're all home now.

CHAPTER 6

Notes
From the Heart

.

*R*ick used to email me poems on occasion. When I saw a subject line like "soulmate just before dawn," I knew it was from Rick. So emails hold a special place in my heart and this section is a scrapbook of some of the many emails I receive related to Rick's heroism. Some emails are excerpts from larger pieces, and others are presented in full. The emails range from people moved after reading Heart of a Soldier, or watching a broadcast of The Man Who Predicted 9/11, to learning about Rick in school, coming across the RickRescorla.com website or simply feeling compelled to express themselves on a 9/11 anniversary.

I do not know most of the people who contact me, but I respond to almost all of them, and have had further correspondence and thoughtful telephone conversations with several of the writers. Regardless of the reason why people write, I am reminded of the synchronicity of life. My growing awareness of synchronicity has helped me understand how circumstances one could never have imagined can evolve in ways that result in a significant connection with others. In

107

that sense, the technology provided through the Internet, and the added dimension it offers in helping people make connections, is wonderful. The support, reflections, kindness and appreciation expressed by so many people who have found me through the World Wide Web never fails to lift my spirits.

I have taken the liberty of some gentle editing and provided either a heading or the subject entered by the sender. I have intentionally eliminated the names of the email writers, preferring to let the words stand alone in illustrating how people have been touched by a hero that most of them never met.

What A Second Grader Taught Me

I am a second grade teacher in a small town. Today one of my students came to me with a story she had written about the World Trade Center. We had discussed the events of September 11th, but this student took a special interest in learning more about what really happened that day. The child came to me with a story about Rick Rescorla. She wrote about what a hero he was and how many people he had saved. Apparently she saw a special about him on TV and was so moved about what she saw that she wrote about it.

In order to help her finish her story, the child and I completed some research about Rick together. I was so touched by his story. This child and I spent a lot of time looking at pictures and articles, and soon many of my students were gathered around the table to hear the story as well. Most of these children were not born when these terrible events occurred, and they love hearing about Rick and what a hero he was. His legacy continues to live on, even in a small town.

I Haven't Forgotten Rick

God Bless Ya'll, and I know God has blessed Rick. If not Rick, then no one goes to heaven.

An Honor To Know Of Such A Man

I am a retired New York police officer, participated in the 9/11 clean-up, had a best friend who was in the building during the bombing and dated an FDNY fireman at that time. I can say that the residue of emotions I felt was probably one of the most turbulent that I can recall. With that said, I can't imagine having such a caring husband and then knowing his nature of "above and beyond the call of duty," and wondering where he was and what his status was.

I send my heartfelt condolences as well as tons of respect and admiration for Rick Rescorla, whom I knew nothing of at that time. While everyone was going crazy running from funeral to funeral, the one that most stands out as a selfless hero is his story. A man who took it upon himself to go out of his way and lay down his life for his fellow man, without being paid to do so.

My neighbor, who is an ex-military man, first mentioned Rick to me, and forwarded his bio along with his story. I recently caught his story on cable TV, and it was just unbelievable. I thank you Rick Rescorla for all of your due diligence that came from your humanity, and I bless you, Mrs. Rescorla, for having to live through such a tragedy.

He Saved My Cousin's Life

I'm sorry that it has taken me so long to send you this message. I would like you to know that your husband Rick helped save the life of my cousin, who worked in WTC 2, 67th Floor on 9/11. If Rick had not done the regular drills, I don't know if my cousin would have realized that something was very wrong when he saw papers flying around after Tower 1 was hit. My cousin made it to Sky Lobby 44 on Tower 2 when it was hit by United Airlines Flight 175. Your husband was on Sky Lobby 44 when the plane hit. He was on his bullhorn reassuring everyone that everything was going to be OK. As a result of your husband's reassuring words, my cousin was able to make his way to the stairwell and save his life. Your husband is a true hero of 9/11. And don't you ever forget that.

The Heroes Tale Is Tragic

On this day, we mustn't morn, we mustn't shed a tear; but we must follow along the trampled ground left by the heroes that came and fell before us. We will never forget, but not in sadness. We will hold those dear to us in memories of how they left us, yet through their strengths we shall become strong. Through their sacrifices, our children laugh and drink the sunlight of a promising tomorrow.

The heroes tale is tragic . . . his songs shall be sung forevermore. Hail Rick Rescorla!

A Part Of Me

I was the officer who responded to your home to get more information on Rick while he was missing. You were upset, yet so proud of your husband. I tried to comfort you with words of encouragement but feared the worse for you, your family and friends. You told me of Rick's heroic service in Vietnam, which I did not know of at the time. Your lives remain part of mine, have guided me and will be a part of me for the rest of my life. On 9/11 anniversaries, television programs or someone asking what was I doing that day, your lives remain part of mine, and I like to think I am the better for it. THANK YOU.

All That Is Good In The World

You do not know me but I am writing you from Cornwall and would just like to say that we are thinking of you and your loss today. Rick was a true hero and will not be forgotten in this his homeland of Cornwall. He, like so many who perished that day will not be forgotten, but to us here in Cornwall he represents all that is good in the world and we are proud of our beloved hero, an all around nice guy. I hope this is of some comfort to you on this day.

I Turned 12 On 9/11

I turned 12 on 9/11, so it was a sad day for my family. Now that I have found out what your husband did I feel better because of all the people he saved. I thank him.

May He Rest In Peace

He was a bright and brave man, a giant in the security industry, a giant to the people that loved him and the people he helped save. He will always be remembered. I work for corporate security in downtown New York and his influence is tremendous. A true hero. May he rest in peace and God bless his family.

So My Son Will Understand

I recently completed James Stewart's book, about your late husband. I wanted to let you know that it had a great effect on me and I wanted to thank you for helping tell his story. I was up on the 105th floor during the first bombing in 1993, and was on the 25th floor on September 11th. I was the only one of my relatives that made it out that day, as I lost two cousins. As I read about Rick, I was hoping that he had survived somehow, and was saddened as I got to the end of the story. It is a sadness that I can relate to.

Thank you for sharing his extraordinary life. I have a son who is 13 years old and I am going to have him read the book to understand the horror of war. Thank God for men like your husband, I hope my son can emulate his example of courage and leadership in his life.

Inspired By Rick Rescorla

I am a college student who stumbled upon your husband's story doing research for my Intelligence and Homeland Security class. It amazes me that he found risk areas and predicted flaws in the system that could lead to the 1993 and 2001 attacks. Many Americans have a false sense of security and think nothing can ever happen to them. From what I gather, Rick was one of those few individuals that never took anything for granted even when everyone around him felt safe. His security measures are, for lack of a better word, just about perfect for the situation. The world would be much safer with more people like him.

His leadership in a time of tragedy seems remarkable too. I read anecdotes about him singing to employees while they were filing out of the tower. I am sure everyone around him felt safer and is thankful that such an intelligent man and more importantly, such a heroic man was there for them. It is rare to find an intelligent and careful person who thinks of others in a crisis. It is clear that he planned the evacuation precautions for his company with each employee's safety in mind. After this truly incredible story, I felt like I had to write you. Rick's story is inspiring. I hope I can do my job — and that little bit extra — as well as him in the future.

Make Death Earn Its Keep

Coming up to the 9th anniversary of Rick's final act of valor I just wanted to give you my thanks for sharing his story with the world. I consider him more of an American than most citizens who drew their first breath on this soil. His story is both inspiring and heartbreaking at the same time. You know I think it's important to note not just how a person died but in what manner they faced their fate. I can only pray to God that I have the courage to man up and confront it like Rick did and charge headlong into its clutches, making death earn its keep for the day. May God continue to bless you until you and Rick are united once again.

One In A Million

I admire Mr. Rescorla and the men who fought with him. I am so sorry that such a great man was taken the way he was. It breaks my heart he survived Vietnam only to be murdered. I would have liked to have met him. Rest in peace Mr. Rescorla, you will not be forgotten.

Commuting To NYC

Rick and I had great fun commuting each day from Convent Station to Two World Trade Center. I discovered early on that he was extremely knowledgeable of all the Shakespeare plays and English poets. As I had majored in English Literature myself in college, we had much fun quizzing each other as to authorship and the ability to complete lines of poetry initiated by the other party. I had taken great pride in my ability to compete, but was soundly defeated by Rick's vast knowledge and lightning-quick recall.

Rick was a delightful and light-hearted person. He never discussed his heroic service in Vietnam, so I was totally surprised later when I read books about his actions there. When I read about his actions on 9/11/2001, I was deeply saddened but not at all surprised by his self-sacrifice on behalf of his many co-workers. He was obviously fearless and put the lives of others before his own life. I feel honored and privileged to have known him as a friend. His life should serve as a fine example for all of us. We will miss him greatly. Not too long ago I was serendipitously surprised and pleased to learn that Rick's wife had moved less than 200 yards from me. It is wonderful to have her nearby, not only as a friend, but also as a spark to ignite my memories of Rick.

A Very Brave Man

I am so pleased to find your web site. I read the story about your husband in the weeks following 9/11. His words have resonated through me since then. I remember how he worried after the great life he had lead, that he would just go out one day after another cup of coffee (succinct version). Rick was a very brave man, an AMERICAN HERO! I know you are so proud yet I am sure you miss him every day. God Bless you. I promise — we will NEVER FORGET!!

Love And Prayers

I work in a storage area where a beam from WTS is stored. Just last week, while kneeling at the beam, I prayed for closure and peace. My son, currently at Ft. Bragg, will deploy to Afghanistan in June. When I awoke to the news of the Navy SEALs raid and they got Bin Laden, you were the first thought on my mind. This long awaited event will not bring back all that lost their lives on that day, but I hope it will lift a huge weight and allow families to feel some justice. I think of all the strong and brave ladies I admire. You and Julia Moore are the women I admire the most, ladies who stayed strong during terrible times and have made a difference.

Watching *The Man Who Predicted 9/11* Again

I just got done watching *The Man Who Predicted 9/11* again. I have my own copy, and I watch it each 9/11 to never ever forget what happened that terrible day. I just wanted to let you know I was thinking about you and hoping you are OK.

In Our Thoughts Today

You do not know me, but I am a radio presenter in Penzance, Cornwall. I would just like to say we are thinking of you and your loss today. Rick was a true hero and will not be forgotten in this, his homeland of Cornwall. He, like so many who perished that day, will not be forgotten, but to us here in Cornwall he represents all that is good in the world and we are proud of our beloved hero and all around nice guy. I hope this is of some comfort to you on this day.

I'm Not A Religious Man

I just wanted to send you a quick message of support for the coming days. Obviously nothing can bring back those nearest and dearest to us, but at this time I just wanted you to know that there are people all over the world thinking about those who were lost in the terrible events of 9/11.

I hope you can draw strength from the knowledge that the world will never forget what happened that day and the sacrifice that was made. I'm not a religious man personally, but I'll be lighting a candle on Saturday for all those lost and I'll be thinking about Rick.

A Man Like Rick

I'm sorry if my email conjures up any bad memories. I lost five friends that day. One, a firefighter, was very close to me. For the past eight years since that day I have always felt in my heart that I should have done something better with myself. The time was never right. I had a great job, girlfriend etc. Now the time is perfect.

I was a mere 22 years old when I escaped the World Trade Center on 9/11. I worked at Morgan Stanley. I did not know Rick, but as a Morgan Stanley alum, native New Yorker, and American, I have come to love and respect him and the heroic man he was. I am now 30 and fed up with Wall Street.

I look at a man like Rick and think that I should be doing something better with my life. Soon I leave for Ft. Benning, Georgia, as I have joined the Army and am going to Officer Candidate School. My goal is to be an infantry officer in the Airborne and then to serve in Afghanistan. The saying goes that revenge is a dish best served cold. I hope to get mine in due time. I will be thinking of Rick and all of those who suffered the same fate as he did on 9/11.

Singing As He Organizes Heaven

I knew of Rick from the Nam. I served with the 12th Cavalry in '66 and '67. While in the field we talked of prior battles of the various units and the Ia Drang always came up and the leaders. Rick was remembered as the best platoon lieutenant. And Hal Moore as the best battalion commander.

I now work for the Air Force. I was the first in our building to hear of the attack on the Trade Center buildings. We managed to get the closed circuit TV to pick up the outside. We watched in horror knowing that we are now at war as one and then the other tower fell. Days later I read through the list of missing person's and was shocked when I found Rick's name. I found CNN's memorial page and wrote a note. I printed the picture and hung it on my cube wall here to remind me of a hero and why we are fighting. I hurt every time I think of Rick and just know that he is singing in heaven as he gets it organized. He has blessed us all in his life.

California Cornish Cousins

It is with sorrowing hearts that we mark another sad anniversary for the murders at the Trade Center in New York. We are California Cornish Cousins, founded to stimulate interest in Cornish culture, and like Rick, we are proud of our Cornish heritage. I, along with many other Cornish Americans will always remember your remarkable husband and our hero, Rick, especially on this day.

A True American Hero

It was because of 9/11 that I joined the Army. I was deployed to Afghanistan and the name of our FOB is FOB Rescorla. I didn't know about Rick and then read *Heart of a Soldier*. Upon completion of the book I now have such a great respect for him and his family. He was a true American hero. My family and I owe him so much. I want to let you know that he is not forgotten.

My Big Brother In Spirit

You have never met me and to my regret I have not communicated with you over these last eight years. I worked for Rick in the Morgan Stanley offices in San Francisco. I was the security manager for the West Coast reporting up to Rick.

I have wanted to say for a very long time how deeply sorry I am for your loss and for the world's loss of Rick Rescorla. Although Rick and I never had lots of face time together, the few times he flew out to see me made me realize that he was a man of humility, sincerity, great knowledge and a spirit to give back more than he would take. A truly loving and beautiful human being, father and husband.

My interaction with Rick was more of a big brother giving great advice to me than a boss giving commands to a subordinate. There was nothing that Rick would hold back on and his clarity and candidness of thought was such a refreshing change from other directors before and since. As I have stated, Rick is my big brother in spirit and I have mourned for him and his family daily.

September 10th at approximately 10:00 a.m. was the last time that I spoke to Rick. I had called him to discuss new security measures, policies and hardware for our San Francisco offices, as the security access control systems were antiquated. Rick was always conscious of holding costs down and doing more with less. During the course of our conversation Rick was suddenly called away to respond to an emergency situation and had to cut the call short. Rick quickly summarized what he wanted for me to carry out and his words were not only directed to our subject matter but also startlingly prophetic: "Security is a behavioral science, not a hardware issue."

That sentence was so sharp, direct and exact that I immediately wrote it down. If you could have seen me at that moment I probably looked like I had just been enlightened from above. I have been to seminars and meetings that took hours and even days that did not have the content of that sentence. Please know that Rick is in my prayers and his greatness is now eternal.

I Still Can't Understand

I've just seen the History Channel program about Mr. Rescorla. Even nine years later, I still can't understand how people can do things like that. I would like to express my real feeling of respect about Mr. Rescorla, understanding that he lived his life trying to save people. Very few persons in the world have this kind of feeling.

Deepest Thanks From A Stranger

I am still consumed with the events of 9/11, reading and viewing whatever I can get my hands on. Quite obviously, within those words and pictures, the name of Rick Rescorla and his incredible heroism has surfaced on numerous occasions.

I am writing simply to offer my deepest appreciation for all that your husband did for New York and for this country, both long before the events of 9/11 as well as on that horrific day. There were many heroes that day, of course, but from what I have seen and read, Rick was one extraordinary kind of hero, the likes of whom may never again be seen during my lifetime, perhaps even never.

As I watched the events of that day unfold on TV, I knew we would all later hear of heroes, those who were called for a far more difficult task that day than most others were. It was not that much longer before I heard about the passion of your husband to save the lives of so many ordinary people who were there at the towers on that fateful day.

My dad, a WWII veteran stationed in England, came to New York City frequently on business for some 30 years. I thank God he died a few years prior to 9/11, so he never had to watch that horror. I had many dinners with him in NYC. My brother was a marine, four years in Vietnam. We all owe your husband an extraordinary debt of gratitude for the many lives he saved that day.

I hope that his loss has become somewhat less difficult for you to bear as the years have gone by. You always must have known that he was an unparalleled hero long before 2001. Now, the whole world also knows. I suspect that you must be an extraordinary woman to be the wife of a man like Rick, and I do hope that you will accept a strangers deepest thanks for the ultimate gift he gave to our city. You are both always in my prayers.

Happy Veteran's Day

We will not forget what a true American hero is. I just hope I could be 0.1 percent of the man he was.

God Took Him First

This September 11th my 7-year old son and I watched *The Man Who Predicted 9/11* on the History Channel. My son has always viewed life a little bit outside the mainstream and has had some difficult diagnoses. However, his words are often stunning.

As you know, near the end of the show, it talks about how Rick went back inside to rescue others even though he could have stopped. It also stated how the building collapsed on top of him and how his body was never found, but other bodies were. After watching the entire show and not saying one word, my son said, "I know why they never found his body." I asked "why?" and he said: "Because God took him first."

4RICKR

I have been an admirer of Rick's (and of yours) for many years ever since reading about him in James Stewart's article. I have been trying to contact you for a long time. In California, we can have "personalized" license plates. My license plate has been "4RICKR" for seven or eight years now, in honor of Rick. Everybody who sees it for the first time asks, "what does that mean?" My response is always "do you have a few minutes? Let me tell you about a truly amazing guy." After hearing about Rick, they're all in awe — as they should be.

Man Of Action

I live in a small town called Crieff in Scotland. I'm writing this email because a motorcycle club to which I belong to was having a discussion on 9/11. My only contribution was to tell the amazingly brave story of your late husband, Rick.

My reason for repeating Rick's story is that I feel we should not waste time and words talking of conspiracy theory's, but that we should remember and give thanks for those whose insight, thoroughness and unrivaled bravery saved many, many lives that fateful day, which Rick undoubtedly did.

You must feel his loss everyday and for that there is no solution other than to take great pride in the fact that he was a man of action, not words. Whenever I hear of 9/11, I think of Rick and all the innocents taken that dreadful day. Not without sadness I should add, but also with immense pride and confidence in the amazing things that good and true men can achieve.

121

We have a term for men like Rick here in Scotland, who are truly great men. Human beings which inspire us all with their bravery, dedication and compassion for their fellow men. It is "Some-man." Rick Rescorla was most definitely "Some-man." He is gone from us now, sadly and may he rest in peace. But, the self-sacrifice of his life in his continued attempt to help others will never be forgotten. At the going down of the sun and in the morning, we shall remember him.

I Will Never Be The Same

I wanted to let you know that I am so thankful and proud of what your husband did for our country. I heard about him in my Accounting information class. My professor was talking about having good security measures in place and practicing what you would do in case of an emergency. She said her son is or was stationed in Afghanistan at a place they called Rescorla. She didn't know the details around it but researched it.

She shared your husband's story with our class and I will never be the same after hearing it. What a dedicated person. I know the employees of Morgan Stanley must have been so tired of going through the drills every month, having to leave their desks, etc. but wow, I bet they are thankful for what your husband did. What a display of unselfishness. We all can learn a lot from him.

Troopers Will Know

I would like to set up a memorial for Rick here in the squadron headquarters. I saw the documentary on your husband and was completely floored that my unit has the privilege of service in the 7th Cavalry such as your husband. I had heard of his actions as an outstanding trooper in the 7th Cavalry, but not from his actions on 9/11. The troopers here need to know of him and pay their respects.

Thinking Of You

We are thinking of you and Rick . . . a beautiful, sunny, warm, summer day in New York City. We hope you and the family are well. As usual, I will venture up to Saint Patrick's Cathedral to light some candles, especially for our hero, Rick, who I am sure is looking over all of us. God Bless You and Rick. As I always say: Rick is still with us . . . he is just not present.

Nine Years Later

You do not know me, but I am a friend of a Norwegian knifemaker who was friends with your husband. My friend met Rick at a knife show in New York and they became friends. I was at my friend's house the morning of 9/11 in Bergen, Norway. My wife and I drove down to Kristiansand and it was there that I heard about the attacks. I called my friend, and we talked about what was happening and about Rick.

In 2003 my wife and I went to New York from California, meeting my friend from Norway and his wife. We went down to Ground Zero to honor Rick and those that had fallen. I never met Rick, but from what my friend has told me, I just wanted you to know that 9 years later I still think of Rick and honor his memory. I just wanted you to know that there are others out there who you have never heard from that think of Rick. I am sorry for your loss, and I hope my words can be of some comfort to you.

Your Husband's Heroics

I will not bother you on Saturday, so I am sending just a few words now. I will be joining millions of Americans in remembering the tragedy nine years past. I just wish more knew about your husband's heroics that day.

Proud To Have Fought

I just finished reading a segment in my textbook about Rick Rescorla for my Military Science class for ROTC. I became upset reading it and wanted to find out more information. I found the web page and am just so extremely proud of Rick's accomplishments and life, and find courage and strength in it. I graduated from The Citadel in 2003 but came and enlisted after a few years of the civilian world. I am now stationed in Hawaii going through the ROTC program to attain my commission.

I really just wanted to say that I thoroughly enjoyed reading about all this and am upset I did not know of him earlier. It makes me even prouder to be an American and to have fought in Iraq in 2007-2009. I will keep you and your family in my prayers and thank you for sharing Rick's success before his death and after his life. I am honored to serve and wear the same uniform for a fallen brethren in arms. "We few, we happy few, we band of brothers, For he to-day that sheds his blood with me Shall be my brother."

The Cards We Are Dealt

I wanted to say what a great read *Heart of a Soldier* was. I was riveted and moved deeply. I am a 53 year old ex paratrooper and was so touched in so many places by the love and growth of his life. It was a reflection of life itself. You are dealt tough cards many times, but we have to do what we have to do. My son is interested in the service very much, and

I want him to read this book before he goes in to make sure he knows all sides of valor and honor, plus the crosses one may have to bear for duty served.

Remember Rick Rescorla

I am a high school English teacher. On 9/11 I read Mr. Rescorla's story to students. We discussed his action and what it means to be a patriot. I posted and left up a photocopy of the picture of Mr. Rescorla in the la Drang Valley. It was interesting to me, as this may be the last set of students to come through my classroom who actually have any 1st hand recollections of that day.

When I began teaching here, one of my concerns about our school (which has over 2,000 students) is that we seemed woefully unprepared for any disaster. Our new principal shared that concern and we are finally having, today during 6th period, our first set of disaster drills. All day long I have reminded students to "Remember Rick Rescorla," and then asked them what I mean by that. Happily, most students are able to recall who he is (frequently pointing to his photo on the wall) and what he did that fateful day eight years ago.

They have also been able to interpret what I mean when I tell them to "Remember Rick Rescorla," that I am making a plea to them to take the drills seriously. Fortunately, I believe that my students will largely take it seriously, especially after I additionally remind them that here in California, we don't have earthquake drills "in case" there is an earthquake. It's for "when" we have an earthquake!

We are keeping Mr. Rescorla's memory alive, and using him as a reminder that our safety is in our hands as we anticipate those terrible things we pray never befall us.

What Does It Take?

As an employee of the Department of Homeland Security, I have tried for almost 10 years to spread the news of Rick Rescorla's heroic act of selflessness on 9/11. My wife and I have signed the Presidential Medal of Freedom petition for Rick, originally sent to President Bush, and now to President Obama. The memorial at Ground Zero would have almost 6,000 names on it had it not been for Rick Rescorla.

I Wish He Could Have Come Home

I am sure I am just one of hundreds of emails you receive. My husband was a Marine and did tours in Vietnam, retiring after 20 years. My Dad was a four-year Marine and my brother and our son was a Marine for over 10 years until he was disabled in Iraq. So you see, I have the utmost respect for military personnel, police and firefighters.

For your husband Rick and all the men and women who serve our country I am humbled. I get tears each time I see the story of your husband. My husband and I have had many conversations about 9/11, but especially comparing the thought process Rick had and how it compared to my husbands, since they shared military experience. Thank God for Rick and all he did. So many will never know what a wonderful human being he was. You are so blessed to have had him in your life, I just wish he would have been able to come home to you . . . that is my sadness for you. Continue to love and keep Rick in your heart . . . it will make each day a bit better.

CHAPTER 7

Opening Up
to Life

I serve on the board of directors of my friend Nick Snider's National Foundation of Patriotism, and ran into someone associated with the Foundation while attending a recent meeting in Atlanta. I met the man briefly several years ago, but he made a comment that both comforted and startled me.

"You have a certain glow to your presence, and I think it is because Rick is beside you," he said.

I think he was right, as my sense that Rick's spirit is with me is a feeling that has remained, which comforts me.

Like many murdered on 9/11, Rick's body was never recovered. Several weeks later I held a memorial service for him. Rick had introduced me to the Raptor Trust, in nearby Millington, one of the largest bird rehabilitation centers in the country, and is recognized as a national leader in the field of raptor conservation and avian rehabilitation. We visited twice before 9/11. Rick was quite taken with the hawks, the falcons, the owls, but especially the American eagles. One cage contained two eagles, Treader and Uno. Some cages had plaques memorializing donors to the trust's endowment, but there was not one on the eagle cage.

Shortly after our second visit to the Raptor Trust, Rick unexpectedly said he had changed his mind about what to do with his ashes if anything should happen to him. Originally he wanted his ashes scattered in a certain area of Cornwall. But now, he emphatically told me he wanted a donation given to the Raptor Trust and a memorial plaque on his behalf placed on the cage housing the American eagles.

When I called the Raptor Trust, I did not know if the eagle cage was still available for a memorial plaque, but fortunately it was. I spoke with Len Soucy, who founded the raptor preserve nearly 30 years ago with his wife Diane. Len came to my house and we scheduled a memorial service for October 27th.

The service was intentionally small as Rick would have wanted, with only his children and mine, and his closest friends attending. At the service, a single bagpiper played beautifully, Rick's son Trevor read a poem *Across the Sea*, and I read the lyrics from *The White Rose* the Cornish song Rick and I loved so much, and several Zen Buddhism quotes. I also read the words I wrote from the plaque:

In loving memory of my sweetheart, my soulmate forever,
my Celtic hero in life and our hero in death.
Richard C. Rescorla, May 27, 1939 — September 11, 2001.
Just like the eagle, you have spread your wings,
and soared into eternity.

There is an American flag flying at the site, and I have since planted beautiful flowers. I am eternally grateful to Len and Diane who are such compassionate people. Len told me how people respond when they come upon the site.

"I have personally witnessed many people who either cry or start looking very sad once they realize the connection to Rick," Len said.

"People understand that Rick Rescorla was a real hero, and I am pleased that the memorial has probably been viewed by as many as half a million people over the past 10 years. We have 80 cages, 60 memorialized, and certainly the Rescorla Memorial is the most famous. We have named one of the bald eagles Colonel in Rick's memory."

I visit the Raptor Trust often and feel Rick's presence, thankful for this quiet place to feel at peace, and remember.

Since 9/11, coping with emotions ranging from shock and grief, to rage, denial and emptiness, is an ongoing struggle. But it is better. Looking back, I do not really know how I made it through the first hours, much less the first weeks, following that devastating day. My wonderful family and friends continued to gather in my home to light candles, hope, and pray for a miracle. The stream of well meaning, but knowingly futile calls of support continued, sometimes leaving me feeling more lost than ever. I often felt nauseas roaming the house searching for necessary paperwork or legal documents.

The first time I tried to drive, I backed my car right over my neighbor's front lawn. I regularly had the company of family, friends, and visits from supportive military personnel, but I insisted on staying alone overnight because that was what I needed to do. A couple of times I could not convince one of my daughters to leave me overnight, but otherwise, I was by myself through the night, with the exception of my dear Buddy.

As dog lovers will appreciate, some of my greatest comfort came from my magnificent, 120 pound Golden Retriever. Rick was not a fan of dogs as house pets, but tolerated Buddy for my sake. He even walked and fed him now and then. Because of Buddy, I was forced to do something besides cry each day since he needed his walk. I'm quite sure it was because of Buddy that I was able to maintain a semblance of composure when someone innocently asked, while walking him on September 12th, if I knew anyone who had been at the World Trade Center the previous day.

I thank God for my Buddy. I think we saved each other's lives. At 14, Buddy had health issues. He could not climb the stairs to our bedroom due to his arthritis, so for two years I slept on the living room couch downstairs and Buddy laid on the floor next to me. On nights when it stormed, he became so upset that I slept next to him on the floor. Buddy was my friend, a constant presence that greatly helped.

Still, by December, I felt displaced and was deeply depressed. I wanted to jump into the pond in front of our house and die. I realized I had to do something to help myself, and I found a personal trainer in the yellow pages who ended up working with me for several years.

Eventually Buddy's arthritis and overall declining health made it necessary for me to consider putting him to sleep. When his kidneys began failing, a person from my compassionate veterinarian's office came and hooked him to an IV bag. I sat, Buddy's head on my lap, while he received his treatment.

I kept Buddy alive as long as I could. Thinking back, I wonder if I was wrong to keep him alive as long as I did, although I remember my veterinarian saying I would know when the time was right to put Buddy down. I can't remember what month it was when that day came, but it must have been warm because we went on my little back porch, which I called my secret garden. I laid with Buddy on the floor, surrounded by colorful flowers and beautiful plants, and held him in my arms as my veterinarian's technician gave him an injection to painlessly put him to rest. Buddy was the best dog in the whole world and I still think about him every day, which is probably why I can't get another dog and never will. He was always there and he was great. I asked Mervyn Sullivan to paint a picture of my Buddy, which hangs on my bedroom wall.

A few months before 9/11, I had fortunately grown closer to a neighbor, Janis Paris, who has since become my dear friend. Janis has been so supportive, and we are quite compatible because we have a similar way of looking at the world. For the past decade, Janis has accompanied me to many of the memorials, award dinners, premieres and other events I have been invited to attend. As Janis recently recalled:

> I remember Rick as this strapping guy who spent Sunday mornings washing his green Lincoln and simultaneously singing (rather fortissimo), songs from his native Cornwall with the enthusiasm of Pavarotti. Passing Susan and Rick on their late day walks, it was apparent they were deeply in love and totally engrossed in each other. Hence, brief greetings and words were exchanged, leaving them to their own private world.
>
> A few months prior to September 11th, Susan and I grew closer, exchanging 'girl talk' about her daughter's impending wedding. Our friendship blossomed. September 11th shattered any hopes of Rick and Susan growing old together — their plans and dreams reduced to ashes. This was also the day that I truly "met" Rick Rescorla. Rick then came to life to me over the past decade while I accompanied Susan to

events, to numerous to count, that she was invited to attend.

What I learned about Rick was this: Rick Rescorla, warrior, writer, poet and hero — who was prepared and ultimately did — lay down his life for the adopted country he so loved and honored. A pragmatist and a dreamer who knew first hand the realities of life yet, still dreamed of a better world. My life has been truly enriched by my friendship with Susan and through that friendship coming to know and admire the man called Rick Rescorla.

Many of the military functions that Janis and I have attended were due to the graciousness of Bob Daniels, the events chairman for the Armed Services Committee at The Union League of Philadelphia, and president of the Brentwood Group, a business development and strategic planning firm. One of the most memorable ones was when Bob invited me to a Union League of Philadelphia luncheon honoring General David Petraeus. In fact, Bob even asked me to bring *Heart of a Soldier* for General Petraeus.

A powerful, striking figure, General Petraeus gave an incredible speech. I was surprised and honored when I was presented with a dozen white roses courtesy of Bob Daniels. As Janis and I were leaving, General Petraeus placed a medallion in my hand which read: For Excellence, Commander, U.S. Central Command. On one side of the bronze coin is a flag and four white stars, and the other side has a red handled saber and green leaf.

Overwhelmed by the gesture, I said, "It is such an honor to have met you. I can't thank you enough for giving me this medal."

General Petraeus replied, saying, "No Susan, it is my honor to meet you."

Janis also accompanied me when Susan Herman, at that time the Executive Director of the National Center for Victims of Crime, who has since become a dear friend, asked me to speak at their ceremony honoring Rick with its 2002 Annual Leadership Award at Bryant Park, New York. Prior to 9/11, I do not think I appreciated what being a victim really meant. I just knew that thinking of myself as a victim injured my pride and removed the illusion I had that I was in charge of whatever happened to me in my life. Certainly Rick would have objected to being called a victim. He would have said it was his choice and obligation to carry out his security responsibilities.

But I remembered when I received Rick's death certificate, with the word "homicide" typed under "cause of death." Prior to that point, I hadn't thought of Rick's death that way. He, like so many others, had died on 9/11, been killed in the terrorist attacks. But the death certificate made me realize that Rick, like everyone that day, had not only died. He had been murdered. Preparing for the ceremony, I began to understand that I, a wife who loved her husband, who expected him to come home the night of 9/11, who expected to live out my years together with the love of my life, was a victim, as a result of the terrorist attacks. In my remarks, I said:

> I was watching a documentary after the Queen Mother had passed away. The documentary pointed out how after Buckingham Palace was bombed during World War II, the Queen Mother said the incident helped her realize what it meant to be an East Ender, a victim. I feel a little like that myself. It's taken awhile, but I've had to face the fact — I am

a victim. I'm one of the innocents, one of the many who lost their lives or dear ones. And it hurts in ways that words can't describe — and it always will.

My healing process has included reaching out to others going through traumatic events. Thanks to the efforts of Retired Colonel Randy Lee, Janis, Dan Hill and I went to the Walter Reed Army Medical Center to visit injured soldiers returning from the Middle East shortly after the war in Iraq began. Many of the men and women had no arms or legs, and we were trying to give them some support. Dan did most of the talking, and I recall he did a good job getting people to laugh several times. We passed out white roses to everyone, and gave them each a copy of *Heart of a Soldier*. Over the years I have sent hundreds of copies of *Heart of a Soldier* to troops in Iraq, Afghanistan and Germany.

I am thankful to Duane Paulson, a retired staff sergeant who Rick knew from Vietnam. Duane suggested I visit the Fort Hamilton veteran's lockup ward in Brooklyn. Fort Hamilton houses many veterans still suffering Post-Traumatic Stress Disorder. Janis and I visited, and it was an incredible experience to sit and speak with these men.

Two years ago, Barbara Lang-Auffret and I again rode with the Iron and Steel riders and we presented a World Trade Center steel beam to the Arlington County Fire Department's Fire Station No. 5, the first responders to the 9/11 attack on the Pentagon. The Fannin County Middle School choir performed songs by Hank Fellows. We then rode to place a wreath at the Tomb of the Unknown Soldier at Arlington National Cemetery. Afterwards, while driving through the cemetery, we came to a sudden stop. Paddy Concannon was in the lead, and saw a woman standing and crying beside a new gravesite. Her son had been killed in Afghanistan. Many of the riders stood with her, saluted her, and tried to offer some comfort before leaving.

Being involved in so many genuine expressions of patriotism have contributed to my deeper appreciation of the bond felt among the 9/11 first responders and everyone who is part of the military family. I also have a better understanding of how people in the military, while often terribly unsettled by the circumstances and experiences they are faced with, find ways to rise to the occasion to meet their responsibilities. I was attending a ceremony where General Tommy Franks was the featured speaker, and remember him explaining how soldiers take a sworn oath of allegiance to the United States and as a result, have a responsibility to finish the job, whether they agree with the mission or not. When Rick went to Vietnam, he knew the war wasn't working, but he had a job to do and a duty to bring his men back alive, and he did the best he could to meet his responsibilities.

As Rick pointed out in *The Prophet,* we cannot police the world. However, when we start something, we must finish it, but it is hard to know how. We have entered a new arena of warfare. There are many complexities involved in fighting people from the Middle East. But as others have said, it is critical to understand that it is not the Muslim religion that we need to be concerned with, but rather the radicals who happen to be Muslim. That is why Rick and many others said we must understand the psyches of these people much better before getting involved, as we are not going to change thousands of years of their thinking and beliefs.

I certainly did not feel this strongly before I met Rick. I lived a sheltered life, a life of privilege. But the terrible reality is that there are people intent on destroying our way of life and that desire will not magically disappear anytime soon. As Rick said in 1998, the new millennium would usher in a new kind of war, a war without uniforms or clear boundaries. Small pockets of terrorist cells have and continue to spread all over the world, and we must continually be prepared to respond to that reality.

Something I learned on my first motorcycle ride to Fort Benning was that many people in other parts of the country think 9/11 happened in New York, the Pentagon, and Shanksville, PA. Despite their genuine sympathy, support and concern, many are unable to grasp the threat to our national security that we must now confront, in part because 9/11 was something they were only able to witness on television. People outside the areas of attack could not really feel the depth of terror that 9/11 struck in people living here.

I remember about a year after 9/11, while traveling to a few states, many people did not want to be reminded of what had happened. As horrible as it was, 9/11 had come, and for most people, been cleaned up and was over, and they did not want to continually be reminded of what happened. While understandable, that attitude will not serve our country well in the future.

But the people we came in contact with during the "NYC to Fort Benning Run" were in awe of the 12-foot, two-ton steel beam. I would hear remarks like, "Wow, the steel from ground zero!" and saw many displays of real emotion from people. It was unbelievable how they were drawn to the steel. Seeing the *steel* from the World Trade Center attacks helped people more fully understand and appreciate what had been inflicted, not just in New York, but to everyone living in our country. I think the steel should be taken to every state to help people understand the potential devastation that 9/11 represents to all of us.

Early on, Rick said the mindset of the radical Muslims was to take their time, that they were methodical, and certainly, from the World Trade Center garage bombing in 1993 to 9/11, that was the case. Today's technology makes implementing terrorist attacks much easier, and given the hatred that radicals continue to harbor towards our country, this new form of warfare will be with us for a very long time.

It is ironic that during the writing of this book, I was woken up by a phone call from my friend Nick Snider to tell me the Navy SEALs had found and killed Osama bin Laden. I burst into tears of joy, and then, like on 9/11, was compelled to turn on all the lights inside and outside of my house. I was proud of our SEALs, and felt an urge to grab the flag from my porch and march up and down the street. But while it is a joy that after all these years, bin Laden is dead, I think most people realize that the terrorist threat remains. Rick warned us years ago about this, and unfortunately the terrorist cells are not going to go away anytime soon. I recognize that we cannot live in a constant state of fear. I continue to regularly visit New York. I love New York. But regardless of where we live, or where we are, we must all be vigilant to protect our country. To be vigilant at all times includes continually raising the awareness of people to the potential threats we face.

Rick had a philosophy about life. He used to say people needed to define themselves, take the time to figure out what they were all about so they could find the strength to keep moving along their path, no matter what happens. He felt maintaining that focus was the way to know at the end of your life if you had done all that you had intended.

I continue focusing and searching as I follow my life's path. When Buddy died, I realized that I couldn't stay in our Morristown townhouse any longer because the solitude and sadness I felt was overwhelming. It was the first time that I had been really alone, having gone fairly quickly from my first to second marriage, and then, within a few years I met Rick. I decided to find another place to live. I didn't look around much, but while house shopping, I remembered something Rick said to me several times within three or four months of 9/11.

"You'll remember me in the petal of a flower, in the ripple of the water, in the leaf of the tree."

At the time I laughed and said, "What are you talking about, you don't know that you're going to die before me!"

When I saw an 1850 Bank House on a property with lovely flowers and trees, a tranquil bubbling brook, and a waterfall flowing from a river, I remember thinking this is what Rick wants for me, and I moved there. And I may move again as I continue along my path. But I now have mornings when I wake up feeling happy. I try and balance my body and spirit with nourishing holistic food, exercise, cherishing the time with my family and connecting regularly with old and new friends. I have another private trainer who works with me on boxing and weight lifting. I have continued pursuing my interest in astrology, and my astrologist has introduced me to Buddhist chanting and meditation. Additionally, other holistic practices, Chi yoga, and Reiki have helped restore my spirit and strength. I also enjoy Zumba dancing, and find it is impossible to be depressed after moving for an hour to the wonderful Latin music. I even have a subtle, but beautiful dragonfly tattoo on my left foot now. I also love riding motorcycles because I feel so free.

As a young man, Rick dedicated himself to a path of adventure, and knowledge, and most importantly, compassion. Rick was distinctive in part because of his charismatic personality. Rick will always be remembered however as a man of great courage, who remained calm in the face of evil. On the day he was murdered, I believe Rick remained true to his path. His heroism saved the lives of countless numbers of people and I am so proud of him. It is my prayer that Rick's story continues to inspire others to find the hero within themselves, and that my story helps people find the strength to heal from the trauma of loss and reawaken to life.

Acknowledgements

*A*s I remember my husband Rick's life, death, and heroism, I want to express my deep connection to all of the 9/11 heroes, the innocent people who died aboard Flight 11, Flight 175, Flight 93, Flight 77, and in the Pentagon, the first responders, and the men and women who continue to sacrifice to keep our country safe. — We Will Never Forget!

I have wanted to write my own book for a long time. I decided now, nearly a decade after 9/11, the time was right to try and remember everything that has happened, and the people who have touched Rick's life and mine.

I am grateful to my family, and my long time and newly discovered friends, and the many people I am not aware of, and have never met, from all over the world who still honor Rick's memory. I am so grateful to all of you. To my daughters, Cristina, Alexandra, and Bianca, their spouses, Kevin Glynn, Claudio Guerrieri, and Brian Bienowski, my grandchildren (Samantha, Cameron, James and Lucia) thank you for being there for me and loving me. Thank you to Rick's children, Kim and Trevor, for always loving and honoring your Father.

I want to say how proud I am of my oldest granddaughter, Samantha, who remembers Rick well, and who unfortunately was watching morning television as the news unfolded and the planes hit the World Trade Center. A few years after 9/11, Sam was taking ice skating lessons and had the honor of skating in a 9/11 remembrance as part of a "Stars and Stripes" skating exhibition on Long Island. Sam and another young girl who lost her dad, skated together, and each was lifted up on the shoulders of a fireman and a policeman. It was very moving and something that Sam and our family will not forget. It was such an honor for her.

Much love to Rick's late mother, Cissy, half brother Clive, his childhood friend from Cornwall, Mervyn Sullivan, his wife Jan, Mervyn's brother Brian, their children and grandchildren, and the Cornish people. It is so wonderful that Rick's family and friends have also become mine. I especially want to acknowledge my love for Rick's cousins, Jon and Sally, and all of their children, Margaret and Chris, Sue and Paul and their family, and my dear special friend Shirley Hubard (sister of Rick's mother's best friend), and Brian Nash. I also want to acknowledge Cornwall's famous water rescue dog Bilbo, who came to a dinner party I hosted in St. Ives, with his master Steve, and my wonderful friends in London, Elizabeth Turner, and her son (Elizabeth lost her husband on 9/11 in the World Trade Center). *Onen hag Oll!*

To Dan Hill, Fred McBee, and their wonderful wives Pat, and Kathy, I value your friendship and help every step of the way, and only regret that I was unable to know Rick as long as all of you did.

I am greatly indebted to Former United States Secretary of Education William J. Bennett for writing this book's wonderful Foreword and inviting me to speak on his *Morning in America* radio program several times.

To Len and Diane Soucy, and the staff at the Raptor Trust, in Millington, New Jersey, thank you for your ongoing warmth and compassion. Len and Diane are extraordinary people and I am so proud that they are my friends, and allowed us to use their sanctuary for our memorial service. To my friend, Ben Montgomery, who lives on the Raptor Trust property. We have had extraordinary conversations and I admire his sensitivity to the rehabilitation of wild birds.

To James B. Stewart, for his ability to movingly communicate Rick's story, heroism, and our love, in both his *New Yorker* article, and his book *Heart of a Soldier.*

I thank David Sandler, who has provided editorial assistance from the beginning of this project, and who I am so proud to call my friend. For the last few years, several people suggested I write my own book. About two years ago, I was able to think more clearly about my experience, began a journal, made an outline, considered where my story might begin and what it might be called, and realized this was a project I could not do alone.

One day, I picked up a New Jersey magazine and noticed an advertisement for help writing life stories by David, a member of the Association of Personal Historians, and whose company, Sandler Communication Services, offers writing, interviewing and editing services. I called David and after meeting, *voila.* Thank you, thank you David. I could have not done this without you. I must also thank your lovely wife Pat, who has accompanied you many times to my house to take notes, and provide a "third ear" and input, that sometimes David and I may not have thought about. Through our many emails, phone calls and meetings, turkey sandwiches, laughter, and tears, David became very aware of the pain and the joy this project was providing. It has been a great catharsis. Again, I could not have done this without David. I know, at the end of the day, I wanted people to know how much Rick touched my life, and the lives of so many others through his heroism, wisdom, and selflessness, and I believe *Touched By A Hero* has successfully captured that sentiment.

I want to acknowledge General Hal Moore, who has spoken at several events I have attended. It has been a great honor to meet you. It has also been my privilege to have privately met with General David Petraeus and General Tommy Franks.

To Rick's fellow soldiers in Vietnam, who followed him into hell so many times on the battlefields, and his Morgan Stanley deputy, Wesley Mercer, and security guards Godwin Forde and Jorge Velasquez, who followed him into heaven.

To Joe Holloway, Jim Kelly, Sam Fantino, Ronnie Guyer, Bud Alley, Larry Gwin, Jim Brigham, and Rick's entire 7th Cavalry, thank you for your never-ending support and friendship.

A special acknowledgment also to the writer Jim Morris, who was co-authoring a script about Audie Murphy with Rick. I also want to acknowledge Sal Mione, Bob Arbasetti, and the New York and New Jersey Chapter of the 1st Cavalry Division, and the many others from that Division for your support.

I am forever grateful to my "Iron and Steel" and FDNY Fire Family Transport Foundation friends. I particularly want to acknowledge United States Air Force Master Sergeant Mike "Bearman" Angelastro, Iron and

Steel Team Director Greg "Spock" Alspach, Retired New York Fire Department Lieutenant Pat "Paddy" Concannon, Danny Prince, Rich Snyder, Mike Stallone. Donny, Gary, Bobby, Mouse, and so many others I can't remember all their names.

My thanks to those who have served at Afghanistan Forward Operating Base Rescorla, Captain Matthew Demny, Master Sergeant Chris Goodrow, Jerry Tiarsmith. Mark A. Kiehle, Brandi, and "mural artists" Brookes and Gardner, for continuing Rick's legacy.

Thank you to all of Rick's OCS brothers including Clarence Renshaw, Bill Foley and Nick Snider.

I want to acknowledge the in depth coverage from the people at the *Mudville Gazette*, an underground newspaper in Germany, who have kept the memory of Rick alive.

To my dear friend Janis Paris, thank you, thank you, thank you for everything.

I also thank my Brookside friends. It took time to get acclimated, and I was lucky to meet the most loving and incredible people who have become dear friends. We watch over each other. I thank Susannah Truitt, Phyllis Florek, Dick Mervin, Joe Mervin, Doug Sears, Craig Dunman, Andrea Turner, Matt Franklin, the people at our post office, library, art studio (especially June Shatken), my friend Michele Zanoni for her healing efforts, the people at the police station, and firehouse, and the beautiful chimes of music played on many occasions by the Brookside Community Church. Also thanks to Bob Zimmerman, a neighbor, who shared the commute with Rick from Convent Station to Manhattan and back.

To my trainers who saved my life over the last 10 years, Tim Sobel, in Morristown and my dear friend and trainer in Brookside, Andrea

Turner, and Rob and Barbara Mason, of Firm Body Fitness in Mendham, thank you for all you have done. To my dear friend, astrologer, and spiritual guide in Florida, Joni Ross, for teaching me chanting, which has been instrumental in helping me focus.

I am thankful to Joe Barrett, a former police officer from Chicago, who worked with Rick at Continental Bank in Chicago. Joe has been to many events honoring Rick, spoke with Rick weekly and is still a faithful friend who calls often.

Thank you to the sculptor Edward Hlavka for creating the outstanding statue of Rick, and to the people at Fort Benning for all they have done. I also thank Carlo Beninati for his beautiful painting that appears on the cover. Sam and Lorrie Fantino who are friends with Carlo requested that he paint something representative of Rick's life, and the original hangs proudly in my living room.

To those inspired to go into security work because of Rick, including Steve Burchesky, US Life Safety Inc., thank you. To the many email writers, thank you for your ongoing support. I also want to thank the Sullivan's, a lovely couple from California who sent me dozens of white roses the first five years on the anniversary of 9/11.

I also want to acknowledge Father Kevin Madigan and the staff at St. Peter's Church in Manhattan for hosting the dedication of Roy Ray's 9/11 Memorial Panel. The first time I saw Roy's exhibition at the Coventry Catheral, it brought tears to my eyes and I knew this would have to be seen in New York.

I also want to thank Bob Erwood who has been so supportive and accompanied me to many events.

I never would have imagined *Heart of a Soldier* being turned into an opera. I am so honored that Rick's life and our love story had its world premier at the San Francisco Opera. I thank the incredibly distinguished people involved including, composer Christopher Theofanidis, librettist Donna DiNovelli, conductor Patrick Summers, director Francesca Zambello, baritone Thomas Hampson, soprano Melody Moore, tenor William Burden, San Francisco Opera General Director David Glockley, and Director of Music Administration Clifford Cranna. I also appreciate the generosity of San Francisco Opera Company Sponsors John A. and Cynthia Fry Gunn, and additional support provided by an award from the National Endowment for the Arts.

To the History Channel for continuing to broadcast *The Man Who Predicted 9/11*, and the producers from Munich, Germany, of *Count Down to Ground Zero*, also shown on the History Channel, thank you so much.

And to my dear Buddy — the best dog in the world.

Please visit the Rick Rescorla Memorial website at:
www.rickrescorla.com